A Practical Guide for New S  *Leaders*

A Practical Guide for New School Leaders

by

John C. Daresh

with

Trevor Arrowsmith

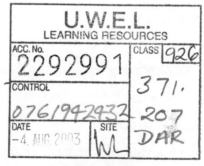

P·C·P

Paul Chapman Publishing
A SAGE Publications Company
6 Bonhill Street, London EC2A 4PU

SAGE Publications Inc
2455 Teller Road
Thousand Oaks, California 91320

SAGE Publications India Pvt Ltd
B-42 Panscheel Enclave #
Post Box 4109, New Delhi 100 017

A catalogue record for this book is available from the British Library

ISBN 0 7619 4243 2
ISBN 0 7619 4244 0 (pbk)

Typeset by GCS, Leighton Buzzard, Beds.
Printed in Great Britain by Athenaeum Press, Gateshead.

Contents

Contents

The authors

John Daresh is currently a professor of educational leadership at the University of Texas at El Paso where he is also the Director of the Principal Preparation Program. Prior to that, he served as a member of the faculty of the University of Cincinnati, The Ohio State University, and the University of Northern Colorado. He began his career in education more than 30 years ago as a teacher in secondary schools in the state of Iowa and the City of Chicago. His involvement with UK headteacher development goes back more than 15 years, when he presented at the BELMAS research Conference in Cardiff, then served as a consultant and speaker for some of the beginning headteacher mentoring schemes promoted by the School Management Task Force, the Welsh Education Office, and numerous LEAs across the UK. He has also lectured at the University of Lincoln, Nottingham Trent, and Manchester Metropolitan. Recently, he became involved as an invited participant at meetings of the National College for School Leaderhsip.

Daresh's publications include more than 100 articles, books, book chapters, and other papers published in the US and UK. Among recent works are *What it Means to be a Principal* and *Teachers Mentoring Teachers*, both published by Corwin/Sage. Daresh has also served as a consultant and speaker in South Africa, Taiwan, Canada, Lituania, France, Israel, Germany, and Holland.

Trevor Arrowsmith has taught English in a number of mixed secondary comprehensive schools since 1979, in London and Northamptonshire, before becoming Principal of a Northants upper school and Language College in 1995.

He has extensive experience as an education consultant, including working on various national headteacher leadership programmes in the UK and Europe, performance management and Ofsted inspections. More recently he has been working on a number of projects with the National College for School Leadership, including Transformational Leadership in Schools with National Professional Qualifications for Teachers (NPQH) participants and the on-line community, talk2learn.

To Stepanie and Bridget

Acknowledgements

The first and most obvious group deserving my thanks is the great number of headteachers now working across the UK and who provide strong and effective educational leadership in their schools. These individuals who never forget the importance of finding ways to improve opportunities for pupils to learn and grow serve as excellent role models and reminders of the best that can be expected in successful schools. While most readers of this book are likely to be at the beginning of their careers as school leaders, others already in the field prove daily that good things can indeed happen for children, despite some of the frustrations found in an educational world so often filled with political, financial and social challenges.

I also wish to give a special word of thank you to my colleague and friend, Trevor Arrowsmith, who has worked so diligently in trying to educate, mentor and keep me on track. His insights into the current realities faced by headteachers in the UK have been greatly appreciated and should make this final product a more usable work.

Many other colleagues in the UK have been most appreciated assistants over the years as I have learned about issues facing school leaders. Among those who come to mind immediately are Trevor Male at the University of Hull, Dick Weindling, and Caroline Sharpe at the National Foundation for Educational Research, Glynn Kirkham at Nottingham Trent University, Linda Ellison at Nottingham, Harry Tomlinson, Ray Bolam, and Geoff Southworth, now Director of Research at the National College of School Leadership in Nottingham. All have generously given me a great deal of their time in patiently trying to explain the landscape of British education as it relates to issues facing headteachers and other educators.

This writing project grew out of earlier conversations with Robb Clouse, my editor for the past several years at Corwin Press in the US. That discussion led to my very productive working partnership with Marianne

Lagrange and her colleagues at Paul Chapman Publishing in London. Marianne's suggestions and observations have been extremely helpful.

Finally, I thank my wife Stephanie and daughter, Bridget, for their understanding as I have spent more hours on yet another writing project. Both have travelled with me on occasion to the UK, and they have both developed a great admiration and respect for our colleagues and friends on this side of "the pond".

John C. Daresh

1

Why Reading this Book Can Help You Further Your Successful Career

Charles Ames had been a primary schoolteacher for about ten years. In the past nine years, he began to move increasingly from the world of the classroom towards management. He enjoyed working with children, and as he moved from management points to deputy headship, he knew he would miss the world of teaching, but he also wanted some new challenges and opportunities for advancement in his professional life.

Charles's dream of eventually becoming a headteacher became a reality at the beginning of the last term. He successfully applied for the headship of a primary school near Nottingham. It is now about five weeks after the current term began, and Charles continues to be quite happy with his decision to accept the headship, but there are now times when the excitement and enthusiasm he felt a bit over a month ago begin to fade. Charles must admit to himself that he might prefer "the good old days" as a classroom teacher.

The single most frustrating thing Charles feels is not that he cannot cope with managing his school. He has a good secretary, an excellent deputy and senior management team, and exceptionally talented teachers. He had a successful experience as a deputy, a post that enabled him to learn many of the management skills that he would now need as a head. What he is concerned about now is the kind of emotional drain that this new way of life is causing him. He knew that there would be conflicts facing him as a head – after all, "leaders are not paid to win popularity contests". He is truly surprised at the number of personnel issues he has to deal with each day. In addition, he now recognizes how lonely it is in his office. Mr Pringle, chairman of the governing body, was very supportive when he confirmed Charles' appointment. Now, however, he rarely comes to visit, encourage Charles, or even inquire about Charles's well-being. Other heads in the area seem friendly enough when he encounters one or another at the local supermarket or an LEA meeting. But his colleagues are also extremely busy at their own schools, with little time to devote to the new headteacher.

All of this makes Charles feel very much a beginner with little connection to anyone or anything.

* * *

Consistent with research conducted in the UK and abroad that predicted shortages a few years ago, there is now a realization that retirements and other factors are contributing to a reduction in the number of headteachers across the nation. This naturally leads to the current situation where more "beginners' are stepping in to lead schools each day.

At the same time that new heads are becoming more common, rapid change is the norm in many aspects of daily life. As a result, pupils are changing drastically, and the management of schools is changing as well as a result of DfEE initiatives and local agendas. The National College for School Leadership is an emerging and vital force in setting expectations of leadership and supporting aspiring and established heads in rising to the challenge of leading their schools. Being a headteacher has never been easy. Events of the last few years have now made a challenging post even more difficult.

On the basis of your experience, list some of the ways in which changes in your surrounding community have changed your role recently. (For example, perhaps many new pupils for whom English is not a primary language have moved to your school.)

....

....

....

....

....

....

If you are not currently a headteacher, you can no doubt imagine how the issues listed above have made the lives of heads different from how they were only a few years ago. If you are a head, you probably already know that these issues significantly affect you each day.

The effect of societal change on the work of headteachers is profound. Thus, traditional patterns of accommodating newcomers to headships are less acceptable. In the past, it may have been possible for newly appointed heads to be told that their job, as the leader of the school, was to step in and learn on the job from more experienced heads throughout the local authority. Such traditional approaches are not consistent with the increased expectations and demands by community members who expect more productive schools. The work of the head is now being examined with a more powerful set of microscopes. Challenges increase, yet opportunities to make the mistakes often seen by newcomers are less acceptable.

This book does not pretend to offer magic recipes to be followed by all beginning heads. No lists of "sure fire cures" will be presented to guarantee success. However, you will read of insights gained by other newcomers and from research related to the needs of newly-appointed headteachers. A great deal has been learned about the things that may help Charles Ames and you as you proceed through the opening scenes of your career as a headteacher. You can look at your new post in two very different, often contradictory ways:

- How to survive the headship
- How to lead effectively

These two objectives are certainly not mutually exclusive. You cannot be an effective leader if you do not survive your first few days in the headship. But there are many who look to the challenge of being a headteacher only in terms of making it through each day. They tend to think only in terms of short-term skills – how to stay out of trouble or even how not to get sacked.

In the following chapters, you will learn of some things that may help to keep you from losing your job or deciding to relinquish it. However, survivorship will be only part of what you learn. The legacy you will acquire here is that of leadership development – how a novice can position himself or herself so that more effective school practice will result. If this stance were not taken, there would be no support here for the best practices of headteachers. After all, effective heads will lead effective schools, and effective schools are what educators have a keen interest in developing and maintaining. You may be a novice head, but much of your leadership and management experience in schools is directly relevant to performing effectively as the key leader of the school.

Plan For the Book

This book reviews many of the issues and concerns often faced by new headteachers. These concerns are described through a framework explained in Chapter 2. A statement of the problems faced by newcomers and some strategies you might wish to follow in addressing these same problems are included.

Later chapters explore other aspects of life as a new headteacher, and each chapter looks at one or more of the major issues faced by new heads. For example, Chapter 9 discusses the value of developing a clear educational platform, or statement of professional values, to guide your work. This is one method of helping you to develop greater awareness of your abilities as you assume your new professional role.

An important part of each chapter will be a concluding section in which you are invited to develop a personal plan for improvement and professional development that is consistent with the issues discussed in that chapter. Through this technique, you will be able to create a professional portfolio and personal growth plan to assist you as you reflect on your first years in the headship. In turn, this information can serve as the basis for a professional portfolio to guide professional growth and development throughout your career in school management.

2

A Framework for Understanding the New Headship

Less than ten years ago, concerns of new headteachers were not considered important by educational researchers. The truth of that statement is readily apparent if one takes time to glance at the literature in educational management over the past 50 years. Many books and articles focus on the role of the headteacher, of course. A great deal is known about the duties of heads, along with the kinds of conceptual and practical skills that are needed to carry out the responsibilities of this educational role. There are even excellent descriptive studies, such as Harry Wolcott's (1973) classic study, *The Man in the Principal's Office*, which provided a rich portrait of depicting life in the "hot seat" of a school leader.

Because of the recognition of a critical need for new people to move into headships across the United Kingdom, however, there has been an equivalent understanding that research on the world of newly appointed headteachers would not only be interesting, but important as a way to inform research of how to establish a method by which one may compare the kinds of issues faced by a newly appointed head with what others have also faced when they first came on board.

Case Study: Working Out the Papers

Cecil Ogumbuzie was in the first two weeks of service as a headteacher of an urban secondary school. He had waited for nearly three years before this opportunity came along. He had spent nine years as a deputy in another school in the same authority, and he was quite happy to look forward to this new role.

Like many new headteachers, Cecil received immediate confirmation of his appointment following a two-day selection procedure. He was introduced officially as the new headteacher of the Rottingham Road Primary School at the evening meeting of the Board of Governors for the school. The next day, Cecil returned to the school to get key documents, and other assorted paraphernalia, mail and notes left by the previous head-teacher. He skimmed over the mound of paper in front of him, and suddenly he began to get uneasy about the new post. He knew from his previous experience as a deputy that a big part of his work would involve keeping records and filling out forms, but he was already nearly overwhelmed by the procedures for filling out reports for the authority, and responding to memos, correspondence, and other paperwork that filled his in-tray. He had had a lot of similar paper to deal with in the past, but that experience was truly minimal compared to what he was now experiencing as a regular part of his professional life.

Case Study: Am I Supposed to Go?

Mary Carter was very happy to become a primary school headteacher in a tiny village in Staffordshire. She was not entirely familiar with the com-munity before she agreed to accept the position, but when she visited it prior to her employment interview, she found the setting to be peaceful and quite unlike the environment she had experienced in her previous post near Manchester. In particular, she was pleased to see the community at a distance, with its Norman church tower and appealing eighteenth century appearance.

The first few weeks at the school were quite pleasant. This was true not only in the school, but also in the community. Mary was able to connect quickly with her teachers, and she was quite comfortable with her new neighbours around her rented house. It was quite near the church that was so visible to those approaching the village. Although Mary was not accus-tomed to attend any church, she felt quite happy to be at a place where so many of her pupils and their parents spent a considerable amount of time in worship each week.

Mary was working late at her school one afternoon when a small group of parents came to her office. They began their conversation quite amiably by expressing their thanks to the new head for the hard work she had already demonstrated in their village school. They were most pleased with the ways in which Mary had made parents feel so welcome each day. But they moved carefully into another topic. It seemed that they represented a larger group of parents in the village who were beginning to feel a bit concerned over Mary's apparent lack of true contact with the village. Specifically, the head-teacher's absence from church services each Sunday and from church-related events was beginning to cause many in the community to wonder if the new head would ever truly become involved in the life of their village. They knew, of course, that Mary had her own opinions about such matters, but the representative parents expressed their belief that it would be important for Mary to demonstrate publicly her respect for local norms and practices.

After the group left, Mary sat back in her office chair and began to wonder what she was supposed to do. She had never been a "church-goer," and what did that have to do with her ability to lead a school anyway?

Case Study: I'm Not a Politician!

Karen Carlisle had been waiting for the past several years for the day when she would take on a headship of a school. She completed the NPQH while serving as a deputy, and also pursued an MBA degree at a local university. She was interviewed by a number of LEAs before she was given her first chance to serve as a headteacher at a small but well-regarded primary school not far from her home. She was extremely happy as the next term approached, and she got ready for the arrival of her staff and pupils.

Karen was especially looking forward to working with her staff on a daily basis. For many years when she worked as a classroom teacher, she was concerned about the fact that headteachers seemed to be getting further away from their roots in the classroom, working with children. Recent educational reforms in the UK appeared to be having many positive effects on student learning, but the emphasis on Local Management of Schools also resulted in headteachers spending an increasing amount of time in their offices engaged in managerial activity. Karen was determined to make her time as a head an opportunity to focus as much time as possible on teaching and learning matters and avoid the trap of becoming a full-time manager. Not only was this a personal goal, but it also seemed to be an idea that was strongly supported by her governors and the Chief Education Officer of the LEA. When she stated that her goal would be to "take first things first" and work with the people in her local community, the interviewing team all said that was exactly the attitude they wanted to see in their new headteacher.

Things appeared to be going quite well for Karen in her first few weeks as a headteacher. However, about a month into the term, she received a call from Dr Malcolm Tuttle who explained that he was the chairman of a local business partnership organization that had been formed, in part, to ensure that schools would be sensitive to the needs and interests of businesses in the town. It was a very pleasant conversation, and Karen explained to Dr Tuttle that she appreciated his call but, for the moment, she could not become actively involved with too many different organizations in the community, particularly those groups which did not work directly with parents and children. Karen thought to herself that the group represented by Dr Tuttle had very little apparent connection with her world and that her time was better spent keeping to her original goals.

As the term progressed, however, Karen began to receive a number of subtle signs from parents and her governors to the effect that Dr Tuttle's group was not at all pleased by being turned away from her school. Karen began to understand that what seemed to be an incident connected to her world as a newly-appointed school leader was having a more and more negative effect on her daily life as a headteacher.

* * *

These three brief scenarios have been selected to illustrate three classic situations representing the kinds of issues faced by many newly appointed headteachers. In the first case, Cecil Ogumbuzie is a new head faced with the enormous demands of a new job. Papers fill his desk, and his governors seem to want answers to every question "right now". He fears that if he cannot respond to these expectations, he may be branded incompetent.

Research related to the needs of beginning headteachers (Weindling and Earley, 1987) has shown that Cecil's concerns are common. They are often referred to as the "technical" or "managerial" or "transactional" side of the headship. They involve the operational details that provide direction and order for a school. One might even say that these skills are needed to "keep the trains running – on time". Included may be such tasks as making certain that laws are followed, and that policies mandated by the local authority are addressed.

The technical side of the headship also involves properly overseeing and maintaining accounts and the school budget, maintaining effective relations with parents and others in the community, developing periodic schedules of important events and activities, delegating responsibility to others, keeping pupil discipline, maintaining a safe and orderly environment in the school and resolving disputes within the school.

It would be incorrect to leave the discussion of important technical demands of the job without noting that, for many new headteachers, a major stumbling block is not solely the lack of experience of how to do certain managerial tasks associated with their job. In fact, they may be quite skilled at doing some of the things required in their job descriptions. Rather, some newcomers have problems because they lack strong communication skills: they know what to do, but they cannot communicate to others why they must do something. That lack of communication involves both written and oral expression skill. The issue here is that even the best "technicians" with the best ideas and motives for managing the school can fail if others do not understand what is taking place.

What are some of the technical and managerial aspects of your job as a headteacher that concern you in the early stage of your career? (For example, have you discovered that you are not terribly confident about budgeting or the use of technology as part of your daily job requirements?) Are these important, or are you attempting to run the school without using the talents of your senior team and staff?

....

....

....

....

....

....

The second case study, in which Mary Carter had difficulty in reading the culture of her school community, was an example of how important it is for a new headteacher to be able to grasp the nature of subtle signals regarding expectations in a new community. Mary was quite happy at the thought of living in a small village, but she was seemingly unprepared for some of the rituals and expectations that would accompany her new life style. Although a headteacher in a large urban or suburban community can feel free to engage in local community activities or not, it is extremely difficult to avoid the attention of townspeople who regularly note the absence of a "key figure" (the new headteacher) from different local activities. Probably no one will tell Mary that she must participate.

Not knowing about the culture, traditions, and history of communities and schools often hinders new headteachers from being able to do their jobs effectively. This gets played out in a number of different ways. Informal dress codes, participation in staff social events (e.g. parties, outings, etc.), or even how to address the school secretary (e.g. always use a first name, or never use a first name) are all examples of the little things that a newcomer needs to understand. They are a vital aspect of the school culture which an incoming head may wish to change over time. This is part of the "vision and direction" which is central to effective leadership.

List some other examples of some of the local traditions, cultures, or past practices that you have discovered as part of your new setting. For example, perhaps you have discovered that Friday in your school is the day on which the head traditionally joins the teachers for tea in the staff room.

....

....

....

....

....

....

The second type of socialization problems often faced by new head-teachers is found in learning about the culture of the headship as a career choice. This involves learning how heads are supposed to act, what they are supposed to do and what they are supposed to know when compared to other headteachers across the UK. Perhaps the best way to summarize this area is with the question, "So, what does a headteacher look like?"

Many new headteachers become so focused on surviving their first years on the job that they ignore the importance of learning what is going on in the professional world outside their own vision. They are unaware of the critical issues that colleagues are facing. It is amazing to note the number of headteachers who have been blind to issues that were faced by headteachers in other parts of the country. It is understandable that local heads feel as if they must attend to local issues first. However, at the same time, national trends are underway that will eventually affect the local scene. The fact that new headteachers are not being systematically integrated into the larger profession often makes this kind of continuing communication with the "outside world" a serious problem.

In the space below, jot down a few additional items that you have discovered are faced by other headteachers across the UK, and that you must also face in your first few years on the job. For example, have you had to face issues of school safety? How about the arrival of large groups of asylum seeking students from underdeveloped nations?

....

....

....

....

....

....

The third case was that of Karen Carlisle, the new headteacher who was surprised to discover that her work as a primary head would also need to include some time as a link with important groups in the community. She could not maintain her personal image of a principal being involved only with the business within the walls of her school. Although it may not have been a part of her personal vision of the headship, she was learning that certain political responsibilities of her world come with the job.

Researchers have found this viewpoint in many new headteachers. Often, it is connected with becoming effectively adapted to a new role or having an awareness of self. Other examples include new heads who are faced with critical decisions that might be different from their own sense of personal values or even ethics. An example is when a new head is faced with the responsibility of assessing a teacher who, in the judgement of the new head, seems to be having a great deal of difficulty. However, the previous head-teacher may have indicated that the teacher in question is very capable. Are the perceptions of the new headteacher incorrect? Or did the teacher suddenly become ineffective in the last few months? Couple this issue with the need for a newcomer to not alienate experienced teachers and another important conflict for the novice appears.

These issues centre around the image that a person has in his or her mind about being a headteacher. Chapter 9 considers some additional ways in which a beginning headteacher must appreciate his or her new role. It is clear, on the basis of many studies of beginning headteachers, that people often suffer a kind of shock when their personal value system is threatened by the kind of things they are called upon to do by others. Can you think of any examples of how your personal awareness of what you must do as a headteacher has been different from what you expected of that role?

Balance Is the Key

In the preceding pages, we have described some of the problem areas identified by many researchers in the professional lives of beginning school leaders. A review of these broad areas:

- technical skills
- socialization
- self-awareness or role awareness

often leads a person to try to understand and generalize along the lines of deciding which area is most important if one is to succeed. Research on newly appointed heads has consistently shown that all three areas are important. In some ways, that makes your job even harder. It is not possible to simply take care of business by doing nothing more than addressing technical skills for the first year or two, for example. This logic is often heard among novices who state that they want to get established as good technical managers first, with the assumption that they can take care of other matters (e.g. socialization and self-awareness) at some time in the future.

Research related to the critical skills that should be demonstrated by successful new headteachers has looked at the issue of how to address the three areas of concern identified earlier. Different groups of educators were asked to indicate their perceptions of the relative importance of certain job tasks that were, in turn, classified as technical skills, socialization skills, or self-awareness skills. When headteachers and principals with at least five years of experience were asked to rate the importance of individual tasks for success and survival by beginning colleagues, they ranked the three critical skills in the following way:

1. Socialization skills (most important)
2. Self-awareness and role awareness skills
3. Technical skills (least important)

When chief education officers were asked the same question, they ranked the skills as follows:

1. Self-awareness and role awareness skills
2. Socialization skills
3. Technical skills

Finally, those who were serving as deputies or in senior management positions that normally lead to eventual placement as heads ranked the three areas as follows:

1. Technical skills
2. Socialization skills
3. Self-awareness and role awareness skills

These findings suggest something very important about the nature of issues faced by new headteachers. First, some important differences in the rankings show up clearly. Those with no experience yet as head-teachers rate technical skills as the most critical issue that needs to be addressed to be successful. However, as people become more experienced, they may downgrade the importance of technical skills, and identify socialization and self-awareness (coupled with appreciating the expecta-tions of others) as being more critical to effectiveness. Or they develop skills in delegating some technical issues to others. They recognize that although the technical side of the job is important, it does not necessarily mean that it must consume the complete attention of the headteacher all the time.

Second, whatever the differences may be when comparing one group's perceptions with another, no group indicates that any of the three skill areas is unimportant. In other words, experienced heads may not indicate that technical skills are as important as the other areas, but they still include as important the performance of the technical aspects of the headship. Socialization and self-awareness are more important, but no one should assume that daily technical duties should not be carried out.

The key to effectiveness and survival is the development of a proper balance between the three critical skill areas. The daily operations of school must be carried out (i.e. technical skills) along with attention to fitting in (i.e. socialization) and the demonstration of knowing what the job is all about and how it affects the individual person (i.e. self-awareness and role awareness).

Suggestions for Improvement and Professional Development

Some suggestions for activities that you might carry out to assist in your professional development related to the three critical skill areas include the following.

Technical Skills

- Seek an experienced headteacher to serve as a job coach and who can share some tricks of the trade for some of the technical parts of doing your job more effectively.
- Make an agreement with one or more of the experienced heads in your area to allow you to visit their schools and shadow them as they engage in the daily tasks associated with their jobs.
- Consult with headteachers who worked in your school before you arrived to learn about critical local issues. Talk with other key players (i.e. teachers, pupils, parents, community members) to learn about their expectations for the role of the headteacher.
- If you are lucky enough to find an experienced secretary outside your door, or if you establish rapport with some of your classroom teachers, ask

them for their insights into the kinds of technical issues that merit special attention in your school.

- Review some of the practical tips presented in Chapter 4.

Socialization

- Work with your job coach and ask questions about the traditions, past practices and culture of your school.
- Go out of your way to attend lunches, breakfasts and other social events that might enable you to gain greater insights into some of the shared concerns of your colleagues.
- Spend time getting to know the personality and characteristics of the school community. Get to know pupils, staff and teachers as people, not simply as these people who happen to come into "your" school each day. The faster that it becomes "our" school, the better.
- Listen and watch in the ways described in greater detail in Chapter 7.
- Become an active participant in activities and events sponsored by professional associations.
- Learn about the "internal and external" realities of your school. Pay attention to and learn about existing (or possible) connections to social service agencies and how to work effectively with local police to ensure greater school safety.

Self-Awareness and Role Awareness Skills

- Identify a personal mentor in your school or in a nearby school to help you get feedback about your career development.
- Write and then periodically review your statement of personal professional values, or educational philosophy. Further information about this activity is presented in Chapter 8.
- Work with a trusted colleague who will agree to observe your work for a period of time and ask you to describe what you believe you are doing in the job. Compare and contrast your perceptions with those of someone looking at you from the outside in.
- Consider how you will address the personal stress you will face as you try to balance your time between your job responsibilities and your commitment to your family and personal life.

Building a Personal Plan

In the spaces provided on the next few pages, begin the process of developing a personal growth plan, or portfolio, by reflecting on the key concepts described in this chapter and specifying some important goals that you may have related to each major issue. For each goal or set of goals, identify activities that will assist you in achieving these goals. Also note the ways in which you can assess your progress towards these goals and objectives.

You may wish to engage in a bit of "360 degree feedback" as you consider the ways in which you need further skill development. What this means is that, in addition to your own sense of what areas need further development, you might actively solicit feedback from others with whom you work to determine their perceptions. Some of the individuals you might talk to include other heads, your senior management team, classroom teachers, and even your chief education officer and chair of your governing board. Remember that all assessments are the product of individual perceptions. Thus, gaining alternative views will provide you with greater insights, but certainly not absolute truth about your areas of improvement.

Area 1: Technical Skill Development

Personal objectives related to this skill area for the next year:

....

....

....

....

....

....

Some of the things you will do to achieve these objectives:

....

....

....

....

....

....

The ways in which someone will be able to tell you if you have been successful in achieving your objectives:

....

....

....

....

....

....

Area 2: Socialization Skill Development

Personal objectives related to this skill area for the next year:

....

....

....

....

....

....

Some of the things you will do to achieve these objectives:

....

....

....

....

....

....

The ways in which someone will be able to tell if you have been successful in achieving your objectives:

....

....

....

....

....

....

Area 3: Self-Awareness and Role Awareness Skill Development

Personal objectives related to this skill area for the next year:

....

....

....

....

....

....

Some of the things you will do to achieve these objectives:

....

....

....

....

....

....

The ways in which someone will be able to tell if you have been successful in achieving your objectives:

....

....

....

....

....

....

References

Wolcott, Harry (1973). *The man in the principal's office: An ethnography.* New York: Holt, Rinehart & Winston.

National College for School Leadership website. (http://www.ncsl.org.uk). You may wish to review the "Head's Diary" included on the website. It provides interesting insights into a variety of issues, feelings, and solutions to numerous social and role issues frequently faced by both beginning and experienced headteachers.

3

A Personal Leadership Checklist

Bridget Casey was finishing her first year as a headteacher of a primary school in Lincolnshire. For the previous five years she was a deputy at another school in the same authority, and she had the opportunity to learn quite a bit about the teachers, pupils and community members. It was not a great surprise when Bridget was named the head of her current school; she knew the community and the community knew her.

As Bridget moved through her first year she remained quite comfortable with her post, for the most part. To a large extent it was a continuation of much of what she had done in the past, and most things seemed to be running quite smoothly. On the other hand, Bridget often went home at the end of the day feeling as if something was missing from this year's experience. She was not completely confident in how well she was doing as a school leader. She was certain that most people watching her performance would call her effective. Nevertheless, Bridget really wanted to appraise her work.

* * *

Bridget Casey is not unusual. Too often, new headteachers invest so much time in finding their job, getting the term started, and maintaining their school buildings that they have little opportunity to check the effectiveness of their work. Are they doing an adequate job? Or are they simply one step ahead of the next crisis that will land on their desks?

This chapter provides you with an opportunity to reflect on your personal leadership style and skills, as compared with the nature of effective leadership presented in current research. The most important part of this process is the expectation that you will conclude your review of the material presented here by identifying some of your personal strengths and limitations. In turn, these may serve as yet another part of your professional development portfolio. The goal here is not to indicate those areas where you have problems. Rather, you should be clear about the ways in which you might be able to enhance your role as an educational leader.

Critical Leadership Skills

Stephen Covey (1991) has noted several key features of those who would serve as effective leaders, or what he refers to as "principle-centred leaders".

- *They are continually learning.* Principle-centred people are constantly learning through their experiences.
- *They are service orientated.* Those striving to be principle-centred leaders see life as a mission.
- *They radiate positive energy.* Principle-centred leaders are cheerful, pleasant and happy.
- *They believe in other people.* Principle-centred leaders do not over-react to negative behaviour, criticism or human weaknesses.
- *They lead balanced lives.* They read the best literature and keep up with current affairs and events.
- *They see life as an adventure.* Principle-centred people savour life; they have no need to categorize or stereotype people and events.
- *They are synergistic.* Principle-centred people serve as change catalysts, and they improve most situations in which they become involved.
- *They work towards self-renewal.* They regularly exercise the four dimensions of the human personality: physical, mental, emotional and spiritual.

Warren Bennis and Burt Nanus (1985) noted that successful leaders engage in the following five strategies:

1. *Strategy 1: Attention Through Vision.* Leaders develop a focus in an organization or in an agenda that demonstrates an unparalleled concern for outcomes, products and results.
2. *Strategy 2: Meaning Through Communication.* Effective communication is inseparable from effective leadership.

3. *Strategy 3: Trust Through Positioning.* Leaders must be trusted in order to be effective; we trust people who are predictable and whose positions are known. Leaders who are trusted make themselves known and their positions clear.

4. *Strategy 4: Deployment of Self Through Positive Self-Renewal.* Leaders have positive self-images and self-regard that are not self-centred, and they know their worth. In general, they are confident without being arrogant.

5. *Deployment of Self Through the "Wallenda Factor".* Before his death, aerialist Karl Wallenda was said to have become more preoccupied with not falling than with succeeding. Leaders are able to consistently focus their energies on success.

After reading these lists of skills identified for leaders in the recent popular literature, select two or three attributes that you believe others might use in identifying your style as you work as a headteacher:

....

....

....

....

....

....

Now, select two or three skills that you believe may be seen as shortcomings of your style:

....

....

....

....

....

....

In the UK recent discussions have led to the articulation of a vision of school leadership that is tied to the ongoing professional development of headteachers. At the foundation of this vision of effectiveness, a Task Force convened by the National College for School Leadership in 2000 identified Ten Propositions to guide efforts for leadership that will have an impact on learning in schools:

- *Proposition One*. School leadership must be purposeful, inclusive and values driven.
- *Proposition Two*. School leadership must embrace the distinctive and inclusive context of the school.
- *Proposition Three*. School leadership should promote an active view of learning.
- *Proposition Four*. Leadership must be instructionally focused.
- *Proposition Five*. School leadership must be a function that is distributed throughout the school community.
- *Proposition Six*. School leadership should build capacity by developing the school as a learning community.
- *Proposition Seven*. School leadership needs to be future-orientated and strategically driven.
- *Proposition Eight*. School leadership must be developed through experiential and innovative methodologies.
- *Proposition Nine*. Leadership is served by a support and policy context that is coherent and implementation driven.
- *Proposition Ten*. School leadership must be supported by a National College that leads the discourse around leadership for learning.

Another list of critical leadership skills and attributes has been developed by the National College of School Leadership (NCSL). As you consider each leadership area, take time to assess your own performance as it relates to each component.

1. Leadership Skills

The ability to lead and manage people to work towards common goals.

Headteachers should be able to use appropriate leadership styles in different situations in order to:

i. Create and secure commitment to a clear vision for an effective institution
    Your personal level of proficiency in this skill:

    ....

    ....

ii. Initiate and manage change and improvements in pursuit of strategic objectives
    Your personal level of proficiency in this skill:

    ....

    ....

iii. Prioritize, plan and organize
    Your personal level of proficiency in this skill:

    ....

    ....

iv. Direct and coordinate the work of others
    Your personal level of proficiency in this skill:

    ....

    ....

v. Build, support and work with high performing teams
    Your personal level of proficiency in this skill:

    ....

    ....

vi. Work as part of a team
    Your personal level of proficiency in this skill:

    ....

    ....

vii. Devolve responsibilities, delegate tasks and monitor practice to see that they are being carried out
Your personal level of proficiency in this skill:

....

....

viii.Set standards and provide a role model for pupils and staff
Your personal level of proficiency in this skill:

....

....

ix. Seek advice and support when necessary
Your personal level of proficiency in this skill:

....

....

x. Deal sensitively with people and resolve conflicts
Your personal level of proficiency in this skill:

....

....

Headteachers should have the professional competence and expertise to:

xi. Command credibility through the discharge of their functions and to influence others
Your personal level of proficiency in this skill:

....

....

xii. Provide professional direction to the work of others
Your personal level of proficiency in this skill:

....

....

xiii.Make informed use of inspection and research findings
Your personal level of proficiency in this skill:

....

....

xiv.Apply good practice from other sectors and organizations
Your personal level of proficiency in this skill:

....

....

2. Decision-making skills

The ability to investigate, solve problems and make decisions.

Headteachers should be able to:

i.   Make decisions based upon analysis, interpretation and understanding
     of relevant data and information;
     Your personal level of proficiency in this skill:

....

....

ii. Think creatively and imaginatively to anticipate and solve problems and
     identify opportunities
     Your personal level of proficiency in this skill:

....

....

iii. Demonstrate good judgement
     Your personal level of proficiency in this skill:

....

....

3. *Communication Skills*

The ability to make points clearly and understand the views of others.

Headteachers should be able to:
i.   Work effectively with diverse audiences
     Your personal level of proficiency in this skill:

     ....

     ....

ii. Negotiate and consult effectively
     Your personal level of proficiency in this skill

     ....

     ....

iii. Manage good communication systems
     Your personal level of proficiency in this skill:

     ....

     ....

iv. Chair meetings effectively
     Your personal level of proficiency in this skill:

     ....

     ....

v.   Develop, maintain and use an effective network of contacts
     Your personal level of proficiency in this skill area:

     ....

     ....

4. *Self-management Skills*

The ability to plan time effectively and to organize oneself well.

Headteachers should be able to:

i.   Prioritize and manage their own time effectively

Your personal level of proficiency in this skill area:

....

....

ii. Work under pressure and to deadlines
   Your personal level of proficiency in this skill area:

....

....

iii. Achieve challenging professional goals
   Your personal level of proficiency in this skill area:

....

....

iv. Take responsibility for their own professional development
   Your personal level of proficiency in this skill area:

....

....

5. Attributes

Headteachers draw upon the attributes possessed and displayed by all successful and effective teachers in the context of their leadership and management roles, including:

i. Personal impact and presence
   Your personal ability to demonstrate this attribute:

....

....

ii. Adaptability to changing circumstances and new ideas
   Your personal ability to demonstrate this attribute:

....

....

iii. Energy, vigour and perseverance
      Your personal ability to demonstrate this attribute:

      ....

      ....

iv. Self-confidence
     Your personal ability to demonstrate this attribute:

      ....

      ....

v. Enthusiasm
    Your personal ability to demonstrate this attribute:

      ....

      ....

vi. Intellectual ability
     Your personal ability to demonstrate this attribute:

      ....

      ....

vii. Reliability and integrity
      Your personal ability to demonstrate this attribute:

      ....

      ....

viii. Commitment
      Your personal ability to demonstrate this attribute:

      ....

      ....

Key Areas

National Standards for Headteachers have been identified by the Department for Education and Employment (DfEE, 1999) and the revised headship framework promoted by the National College for School Leadership has included the following key areas. You may wish to review these statements periodically to assess your personal progress towards refining leadership.

1. Strategic direction and development of the school. Head teachers, working with the governing body, develop a strategic view for the school in the community, and analyse and plan for its future needs and further development within the local, national and international context.

2. Teaching and learning. Headteachers, working with the governing body, secure and sustain effective teaching and learning throughout the school, monitor and evaluate the quality of teaching and standards of pupils' achievement, and use benchmarks and set targets for improvement.

3. Leading and managing staff. Headteachers lead, motivate, support, challenge and develop staff to secure improvement.

4. Efficient and effective deployment of staff and resources. Headteachers deploy people and resources efficiently and effectively to meet specific objectives in line with the school's strategic plan and financial context.

5. Accountability. Headteachers account for the efficiency and effectiveness of the school to the governors and others, including pupils, parents, staff, local employers and the local community.

As was the case with the other descriptions of important leadership skills, you may wish to list here some areas where you will focus future professional development activities.

Your Personal Plan

An assessment of your leadership skills can serve as an important foundation for a personal portfolio and growth plan. This chapter included several different frameworks that have been developed to assist people in analyzing certain research-based competencies needed to lead schools. You may wish to consider these skills, or you may wish to consider other issues that you will need to face as a headteacher. For example, how effective are you in seeking and securing additional resources for your school? After all, a reality of present-day education is that it will be increasingly important for educators to become grant applicants, because traditional sources of financial support are rarely sufficient to allow schools to reach many targets and goals. Other kinds of skills and abilities may also come to mind.

In the space below, identify some of your strengths and some of your limitations with regard to the leadership skills and attributes identified throughout this chapter. For each item, identify a timescale that you intend to follow in either strengthening a skill or finding ways to increase your personal effectiveness. Note also some of the activities or strategies you believe may assist you in your improvement effort.

....

....

....

....

....

....

References

Bennis, W. G. and Nanus, B. (1985). *Leaders: Strategies for taking charge.* New York: Harper and Row.

Department for Education and Employment (1999). *National standards for headteachers.* London: DfEE.

National College for School Leadership website. (http://www.ncsl.org.uk)

Revised National Standards for Headteachers.

4

Expectations for Technical Skills

Neville Grayson stood at the front of Prescott Secondary School and suddenly realized that he was now the headteacher of this school. This was a job that he had looked forward to for quite some time. Last spring, Neville had applied for four headships that were advertised in the *Times Education Supplement*. The schools were all close to where he had been serving as a deputy for the past six years. He went through at least 12 different interviews with governors, parents, teachers, the chief executive officers for four different authorities and community members. In some cases he had done well, and in a few situations he had made errors. When he finally received word that he was wanted at Prescott, he was happy and eager to show that he was indeed the right choice for the job.

Today, however, he started to feel some apprehension as he walked through the front door of his new school. He had learned a great deal during his time as a deputy. He had had a particularly good role model in the headteacher with whom he worked. Neville had got quite a bit of practical information during the past six years. Now he was in charge and responsible for making things happen at his school.

As he settled in at his new desk, he started to sift through the enormous pile of papers laid neatly in his in tray by Martha Quimby, his secretary. She now stood before him, notebook in hand, waiting for directions concerning the order of business to be followed during the next few weeks before the term started. Martha said that one of the first things she had always done with the previous headteacher was to set up a tentative schedule to be followed during the term. In that way, she and Mr Grayson could develop a filing system that they could consult each day to remind them of events that needed to be addressed.

Neville thought that Mrs Quimby had a great idea, but the newness of his job, the thought of being in charge and all the things that had to be done to learn about a new school, a new community, and a new job made Neville realize that he had not given any thought in the past to what had to be done in terms of the technical skills and practices needed to make this a successful year in the job.

* * *

Neville Grayon's situation is not unique. Often, people spend so much time thinking about how to do individual tasks associated with being a headteacher (e.g. how to manage a building budget, or how to pay attention to legal mandates) that they rarely think in terms of the big picture of leading a school for an entire year. School Development Planning, or SIP (School Improvement Planning), are well established in most schools. However, the process and emerging document is valueless if the key issues are not built in and shared with staff and governors at an early stage. What are those key issues?

Alternatively, new heads frequently find themselves in situations much like Neville's: they spend a lot of time worrying about and working towards getting their first job and often walk into the position without really considering a lot of the details involved in what they are supposed to do.

These are both realistic situations beginners often face, and they are concerns not often remembered by experienced colleagues who frequently do things on the basis of their experience.

Some Apparent Contradictions

The most critical skills that must be addressed by any beginning headteacher concern developing an appreciation for personal values and beliefs. As a result, this chapter may seem contradictory, because it looks at the important area of technical skills needed for headteachers to succeed in their jobs. Often, people speak of these skills in a negative way. The implication is that being an effective school leader is something well beyond management. But a person can never serve as a true leader if he or she does not survive as a competent manager. The job has to be done.

This chapter looks at the technical side of the headteacher's job. The goal here is to present an overview of the many tasks that need to be done each year by headteachers and work with you to set up a timetable for carrying out these tasks. Some of these may be classified as mandated tasks that may be required by law or government policy. Other important technical duties need to be done by effective heads, even if they are not officially required.

Formal Requirements

You must do a number of things each year because they are formal requirements of the job. If you miss deadlines associated with these tasks you may be in violation of contracts, policies, or even laws. As a result, these items cannot be allowed to simply slip once in a while. You could lose your job or be held personally and legally liable if you do not meet these deadlines and due dates.

Deadlines are important, but they are listed in formal memoranda, calendars of events, job descriptions, council policies and a wide array of other places that will make them relatively hard to ignore. Few headteachers are wholly unprepared for the fact that, for example, they must report pupil attendance by a certain date. This is an important technical task that you must address, but it is a subtle issue that is easy to forget most of the time.

Informal Tasks

Informal tasks are the things you will not necessarily find listed in local policy statements or in law, or perhaps in the terms of labour agreements with teacher unions. However, failure to do some of these things might make a difference in how you are able to carry out your job as a headteacher. They are the kinds of things that – as experienced headteachers have discovered over many years – make the school term run a bit more smoothly, and reduce tensions and frustrations not only for you but also for your staff, pupils and the community with whom you work.

The next few pages will list some of the important things – both formal and informal – that need to be done throughout a school term. The lists indicate activities that should be performed before the year begins, during the term and towards the end of a school year to ensure that the next year will be easier than this one. Some suggestions fit cleanly into one of these three periods; others do not because they must be addressed throughout a school year.

Before the Term Begins

Although people are appointed to headships throughout a school year, a large number of new heads receive their assignments during the summer, before a new school year begins. In an ideal world, you might be selected as a headteacher in July or August, with your appointment officially beginning on 1 August or 1 September. In that ideal world, then, you might have some reasonable time to plan for the next year, check over your school, learn about the pupils, staff, and community and so on. In the real world, however, you might receive your headship with only a limited time to prepare for this demanding role.

Regardless of the situation in which you find yourself, you can do a number of things before teachers and pupils walk into your school. These activities are classified in several different areas: building preparation; materials and supplies; communications with staff, pupils, parents, and community; and finally, perhaps most importantly, personal preparation.

Personal Preparation

- Continue to read professional journals to learn about major trends in education that you are likely to face as a headteacher.
- Talk to people to learn about special school traditions, events and customs.
- Set up a tentative plan of events for the school term.
- Establish a personal phone filing system on your desk; programme your phone for speed dialling important phone numbers. Set up your e-mail account and telephone answering system.
- Visit a few local experienced headteachers to set the stage for future relations.

Communications

- Send out letters of introduction to parents and staff; invite people to come to the school to meet you. (This is particularly important for teachers who might not know much about you, where you came from, or a lot of information that was not generally known by teachers during your hiring process.)

- Spend time with secretaries, caretakers and others before the school term begins.
- Listen and learn as much as possible about the local culture of your school and its community. Who are some of the local heroes? Are there any legends to learn?
- Meet and get to know the members of your site council.
- Work with experienced personnel to identify local community groups, individuals, or organizations. Do not offend important locals.
- Identify important contact people in community social service agencies, the police and so on. Find time to make personal visits to the people you may need to call on in emergencies after the year starts.
- Form school business partnerships, if possible. Maintain partnerships started in the past.
- Prepare a Welcome Back letter to your parents and students and send it out so that it will arrive about a week before the new term begins.
- Prepare a Welcome Back letter and address it personally to each staff member.
- Do not refuse invitations to important local and traditional events. Every one of these is an opportunity to learn more about the local culture. Show your willingness to be an involved community member and your sincere interest in the people who will be critical to your school's success.
- Prepare daily bulletins and newsletters for the first week of school before the busy first day. Also, prepare the agenda for your first staff meeting.
- Read local newspapers, subscribe to one if you live in another community.

Curriculum

- Learn the teaching culture of the school.
- Familiarize yourself with OfSTED reports and recent national standardized test scores for your school.
- Learn about any special needs programmes that are used in your school.

Building Preparation Activities

The following activities may help you to prepare for your first year:

- Walk around your school with your caretaker and check out the cleanliness and state of repair; note areas needing attention. While making your assessment, develop a priority system to indicate what things need to be done first. For example, are there health and safety concerns? What about things that affect instruction? Facilities for students and staff? Appearance?
- Examine the lighting throughout the school.
- Look over such often forgotten but important areas as ventilation, signs of water damage, plumbing problems and electrical hazards.
- Learn about your building's fire alarm system and security systems and how to operate, override them and disconnect them if necessary.
- Verify that things ordered by the previous headteacher were actually done in your school for the year (e.g. were structural changes, repairs, etc. actually carried out?).
- Check over the external conditions of your school and remember that the premises are what the public sees every day.
- Learn about your school building's idiosyncrasies. This is a particular adventure in older buildings.
- Do whatever you and your staff can to make the school as neat, clean, safe and attractive as possible for the first day of school.
- Arrange your office so that it reflects you and your personal style: move the desk, put up photos, add plants and so on. This strategy tells people a lot about you very quickly.

Materials and Supplies

- Learn the location of supply cupboards, storage rooms and so on.
- Check to see if materials that were ordered last term were delivered; if not, contact suppliers to determine why.
- Make certain that you have an ample supply of paper forms so that you do not run out just as a new term begins.

After the Term Begins

The temptation facing most new headteachers after a term begins is to settle in and wait for some issues to come to you. That will certainly happen. However, you must persist in making a plan that will enable you to anticipate some major events and take developments forward, in addition to anticipating crises that you will face as a new head. Some of these things will take place at the beginning of a term and some will come later. Always be prepared.

Some of the common issues you are likely to face throughout the term in a number of different areas are as follows:

Communications

- Work with local teacher training providers to identify appropriate placements for newly appointed teachers who will be working in your school this term.
- Establish and monitor appropriate parent and community volunteer programmes.
- On a continuing basis, make certain to communicate all important dates for the term to your staff.
- Get to know your deputy and other members of senior management with whom you will be working.
- Develop a clear rota of staff duties and special assignments.
- Share with staff your personal expectations regarding pupil performance and behaviour.
- Learn the local culture of the school as it relates to formal and informal holidays and events. For example, do you have a large number of staff and pupils who observe certain religious holy days each term?

Systemic Responsibilities

- Learn and observe mandated dates for reporting pupil enrolment.
- Work with your governors and local authority to learn procedures for establishing your school budget for the next term.
- Systematically document your personal and professional accomplishments.

Building and Plant Activities

- Keep an eye out for any signs of unusual wear and tear in the school, particularly as these may be related to the health and safety of pupils and staff.

- Make certain that caretakers complete all assignments.
- Use the school building as a symbol of openness and welcome to visitors from the community.

Materials and Supplies

- Make certain that supplies ordered prior to the beginning of the term arrive and are distributed to staff.
- Oversee the use of consumable supplies throughout the school to prevent the interruption of material in mid-term.

Towards the End of the Term

The last few weeks and days of every school term are a big part of your job, because many events tend to stack up and you will need to make certain that they are completed.

Instructional Material

- Survey staff to determine additional instructional materials and equipment that may be needed next term.

Communication

- Distribute a survey to parents to determine their perceptions of the overall programme effectiveness of the school.
- Survey staff to determine their perceptions of the quality of the school's programme.
- Sponsor a special social event (e.g. breakfast, tea) for parent or other community volunteer groups.
- Sponsor a thank you lunch for your office and cleaning staff.
- Share with staff strategies or techniques that might be helpful in the improvement of school practices.
- Work with governors to identify possible priorities to be followed in the next term, building on data collected and analyzed throughout this current term.

Building Maintenance

- Work with your caretaker and cleaning staff to identify work and major improvements that need be done as soon as the current term has ended.
- Establish a cleaning schedule with your cleaning staff so that minor repairs can be made and equipment may be serviced and stored before the school opens again for the next term.
- Check on instructional materials and other needed supplies used throughout the school.
- Involve staff concerning modifications needed in individual classrooms (e.g. replacing damaged furniture, changing lighting fixtures and so forth).

General Management

- Check the master timetable for the next term.
- Check a tentative duty rota for the next term.
- Review staff retirements, relocations, and so forth to determine possible recruitment and hiring needs. Share this information with your governors as soon as it is completed and relate it to the ongoing review of the budget and work on budget projections for next year, or further if possible.

Two concluding observations are to be made at this point. First, the above lists are not exhaustive; they do not include all that you might need to do. Undoubtedly, you will find other important activities in your situation, and some of the items listed may never be relevant to you. Second, no priorities are suggested. You must make your own assessment of what tasks must be done first. But prioritising is a critical task for all leaders.

Building a Personal Plan

This chapter dealt with a review of many of the important technical skills that a new leader needs to master to become a proactive and effective leader. A number of tasks were suggested as possible activities you may wish to carry out before a term begins, after the term has started, and also in preparation for the closing of a school term. As you may have noted a lot of things must be accomplished, but you should not become overwhelmed with the responsibilities of your job. You will need to develop an understanding of major issues that need to be addressed in a systematic way. This type of proactive planning will assist you in becoming a proactive leader, not simply becoming a reactor to the next crisis.

On these last few pages, consider your own situation and identify some important tasks that you will need to address throughout the school year. In listing the specific tasks, make certain that you do so according to priority. Although it has not yet been discussed, another issue that you will need to deal with as a headteacher is effective time management. You will find numerous books and experts available for you to consult in this area, but really, time management means nothing more than making a decision about what must be attended to first. As a result, if you plan to attack several issues throughout the school year, begin here in the management of your time by asking, "What comes first?" After you decide the answer to that question, you may also want to identify specific strategies for carrying out your many duties according to a reasonable schedule.

Before the term begins:

....

....

....

....

....

....

After the term is underway:

....

....

....

....

....

....

In preparation for the end of the term:

....

....

....

....

....

....

Remember that no matter how well you plan, you will encounter surprises and unplanned events, or you may discover some possibilities for which you do not feel terribly well prepared. In those cases, remember that you will never be able to stand totally alone and be effective. Call other headteachers, consult your staff, and gather input from parents and others. After all, you will get a lot more accomplished if you learn to work as a member of a team.

5

Leading as a Deputy

Stephanie Jackson had been a teacher for eight years when she began to explore opportunities for pursuing a career in educational management. Her first step towards that goal was as Head of Literacy Coordinator in her outer London primary school. She proceeded through a variety of management posts in her school, to assistant headteacher. She believed that she was ready to take on yet another new level in her career as a deputy headteacher. She soon found a post in a school, Crenshaw Primary. She was ambitious. Even though she was quite happy to land her job, she was already starting to think of the day when she would be able to begin searching for the job that now served as a major professional goal, headteacher of her own school.

Stephanie's job as a deputy at first seemed almost perfect for her. She grew up not far from Crenshaw Primary. So she knew the community quite well. She was pleased to note that her headteacher would be Ralph Billingham, a highly respected educator who had been at Crenshaw for more than ten years. He was definitely the type of colleague and mentor that Stephanie had wanted to help her in her pursuit of her long-term goal.

True to form, the first few months featured many meetings between the headteacher and his new deputy. Ralph was quite helpful. He would clearly outline his expectations of Stephanie, including such matters as how he expected her to address him in front of staff, and even when he expected Stephanie to arrive at the school each morning. Although she was a bit overwhelmed at first, she was glad to be working with a very strong role model.

As the first year progressed, however, Stephanie became somewhat frustrated in her new post. At times, she felt as if she were little more than a clerk working for Ralph. She spent a lot of time providing cover for Ralph when he went to meetings outside of the school. Another duty was to meet prospective parents who came to visit and learn more about Crenshaw.

Frankly, she had hoped to be able to do a lot of other things that were much more enjoyable. Stephanie also realized that Ralph was doing a number of things that she did not agree with.

"I doubt that this is going to work," Stephanie confided to her friend, Susan White. Susan had achieved her goal of becoming a headteacher only two years ago. She had gone down the same path that Stephanie was now following.

"So you don't like having to do all the work while Ralph gets all of the accolades, eh?" Stephanie did not like to admit it, but Susan had truly captured her thoughts. "Learn how to do all the little things now. They will become much bigger later. Do not fall into the trap of siding with staff or anyone else as a way to discredit your head. Remember that you are a deputy." Stephanie did not really like it, but because she respected Susan she decided to follow her advice.

* * *

In all probability, you have attained your current post as a headteacher after having served in a variety of school management roles over the past several years. Most recently you no doubt were a deputy headteacher for a number of years. While the role of the deputy is not always very glamorous, as Stephanie Jackson quickly discovered, it may have been the most significant learning experience that you had as you prepared to step into your job as a head. The issue described in earlier chapters of this book focused on ways in which you can develop greater confidence and competence in the performance of the technical duties attached to the role of the headteacher. Serving as a deputy can be an extremely powerful way to become better prepared to do the next job you wish to attain in your career as an educator.

In this chapter, some practical tips are offered to you or anyone else who might be serving in the role of deputy headteacher with an eye towards assuming a headship in the future.

Remember Your Role

The role of the deputy headteacher can be a very difficult one to carry out effectively. On the one hand, you are a member of your school's senior management team. Presumably, you long ago made a decision to follow a career path towards school management. On the other hand, you have not yet achieved the role of the headteacher. As a result, you still serve to assist the chief manager of your school; you do not yet have the authority to be totally "in command". But the deputy headship has traditionally been a regular and critical step in the long-term process of becoming a headteacher. You must serve as a deputy, but at the same time use your time wisely to cultivate the skills that can eventually be put to use when you are the leader of your own school.

Using the Role for Your Future

You may wish to remember several things if your goal is to move into a headship some day. Some suggestions follow.

Control Your Ego

No doubt you are a bright, capable, energetic and ambitious educator. Currently you are a deputy headteacher, and you now find yourself with a task which many duties are regularly delegated by the head. You probably deal with many pupil conduct problems. Often, you are the person assigned the task of contacting parents concerning their child's behaviour, attendance, exam scores, or many other issues that can be quite unpleasant. While you do these things, the headteacher gets to stand at the front of groups and may take credit for a job well done. This is often the case when you and the staff did most of the work. But the head gets all the praise.

* * *

Probably, few current or former deputy headteachers have not at least once had thoughts similar to those stated above. Perhaps some things are a bit exaggerated. In other cases, however, the scenario painted in the previous paragraph is spot on. You do the work whilst others get the credit.

The temptation to feel like a victim, or sorry for yourself, is something that truly must be avoided. The position that you hold is that of a deputy headteacher, not "co-headteacher". You were not selected to be the leader of the school. Rather, your duties are carefully defined as a person who will assist the headteacher. This means, perhaps more than anything else, that you must control your pride and ego.

The fact is that you were probably selected because you appeared to have the potential of adding your skills to what is already present in your school. In short, you were selected because people believed you could work effectively with your headteacher.

In the space provided, indicate some ways in which you might face some potential conflict between your own needs to be recognized and the needs of your headteacher.

....

....

....

....

....

....

Indicate some ways in which you might work to resolve this potential conflict.

....

....

....

....

....

....

Assist the Headteacher

Quite frankly, your job is to serve as an assistant to the headteacher. One of the most important ways of providing that support is by assisting the head to achieve success. Even though you are a member of the senior management team, you need to learn to live with the fact that you are not in the pilot's seat. Therefore you may need to suppress a natural desire to call attention to your abilities and accomplishments. You are truly a person "in the shadows".

Several things may happen. If you are fortunate enough to be working with an extremely capable and effective headteacher, he or she will no doubt recognize that you have been quietly and patiently waiting in the wings. Appreciation of that fact may not be demonstrated immediately. But a good headteacher is more than likely to be able to discern competence and a job well done. Your good headteacher was once a good deputy.

On the other hand, you may be working with someone who is less than effective. Continue to support your headteacher and do everything in your power to make him or her look good. Granted, that may be a difficult task, but there are some benefits. First, if you cover for an ineffective superior, you will be doing what can be done to help the staff and pupils in your school. Second, the ineffectiveness of your headteacher is not hidden to others. If you do your job and make things work for an incompetent head, people will quickly realize who is really doing the work.

If you take the attitude that you are stuck with an ineffective headteacher and show that attitude, something else will probably occur. If you don't do the job that the headteacher should be doing, your school will probably look quite poor to those who look at its performance. You will be part of the ineffective management team at a failing school, and your career will probably suffer. Remember that, in many cases, you may not get the particular recognition that comes along with the good things that happen in your school. However, you will probably be blamed for failures as quickly as your headteacher might. People often paint with very broad brushes.

What are some of the ways in which you can increase your status by helping your headteacher succeed?

....

....

....

....

....

....

Keep Quiet!

Whether you are blessed by working with a great headteacher or forced to endure someone who is less capable, remember that you owe your head discretion and loyalty. A big part of those qualities is defined by learning to be very careful about what you say concerning your headteacher. You must not gossip, leak information to others, or above all, disagree publicly with your head. As a school manager, you are already aware of the great amount of material that must be kept confidential. By the same token, you make your work and the work of the headteacher much more difficult by speaking about them behind his or her back. It will be a temptation – if you are drawn into conversation with staff, parents, or community members – to say things that might be understood as critical. The old saying that if others hear you speaking ill of someone, they will begin to wonder if you also speak ill of them in their absence, is one worth thinking about.

You will no doubt find legitimate situations in which it will be necessary to disagree with some action taken by the headteacher. Two words of advice are offered. First, if you disagree with something, say it directly to the head, but not to half the staff. Second, say it to the head behind closed doors. You do not wish to encourage anyone seeking opportunities to "divide and conquer" the management team. When you disagree with something that your head says or does, you have a professional duty to decide if it is of such consequence that you must bring it up, and if you do, to remain discrete and courteous by discussing it in private.

Remember that managing a school is not an enterprise that should be guided primarily by engaging in activities that are directly related to the learning needs of pupils. Having a situation in which a disagreement occurs among members of the management team causes turmoil. It disrupts staff morale and is anything but a good situation for anyone. For the pupils in a school in which such situations exist, it is like having bickering parents in an unhappy home.

If you were to spend time with your headteacher (in a private session) and discuss some of the ways in which you might disagree with tasks that he or she has assigned to you, what might they be?

....

....

....

....

....

....

* * *

Now that you have listed these things, it is up to you to decide if it is wise to share these concerns with the person with whom you now work.

Listen, Listen...Then Listen Some More

The great advantage of adopting a stance in which you keep quiet and control your ego is that you are likely to learn a lot of things very quickly. You can do this through a very simple learning technique that you have no doubt shared with many pupils over the years. That technique is simply to listen and absorb.

A temptation for many deputies is to demonstrate their skills and strengths by taking immediate, decisive action on everything that comes across their desks. There often seems to be an unwritten set of instructions that proclaim, "You are weak if you put off any decision." It is true that many in your school will push you for a quick answer for every issue. And those same people will probably be your strongest allies – if you consistently decide issues to their liking. It is remarkable how "good" managers frequently become very "bad" managers overnight, based on the strengths of making only one contrary decision.

The suggestion is not made that not only making any decisions is good practice. Too often, schools suffer from a type of organizational paralysis that comes from decision avoidance by school managers. But absolute, unyielding and often rash decisions are equally unproductive too. Two things are useful to remember to help you decide the proper balance between paralysis and authoritarianism.

* * *

First, as a deputy you have not only the opportunity but also the duty to defer many of your most challenging decisions to your headteacher.

That leads to a second recommendation for learning about effective decision-making by listening. One of the reasons why your headteacher has the job he or she does is normally because of greater experience as a manager. That probably means that even when you do not necessarily agree with some stances that are taken by your head, it is likely that they have some foundation in past practice. And the only way that you are likely to achieve that same degree of experience is by remaining open to the thoughts of others and listening, observing and asking questions so that you can listen some more. The key here is to adopt an attitude of willingness to learn by absorbing as much as possible.

Of course, the idea of listening as much as possible needs to be tempered a bit by your need to learn as you absorb what others do. This does not suggest that you should never question the reasons and assumptions made by your headteacher. In fact, asking the question, "Why did you take such and such a stance?" on occasion may be helpful to you and also the headteacher. Too often, experienced heads make so many decisions on the basis of past experience that they almost lose track of knowing why they are doing what they do. In some cases, a well-placed and sincere "Why?" by a colleague can be an important tool to promote greater reflection and more effective performance.

* * *

List some of the ways in which you have already learned about being a more effective leader by listening and absorbing from more experienced colleagues with whom you now work.

....

....

....

....

....

....

Ask to Do More

A problem faced by deputy headteachers is that they often get typecast in their roles. They are frequently delegated a narrow range of responsibilities, at times because their headteacher preferred to attend to some matters and personally disliked dealing with such things as pupil discipline or maintenance of the school premises. If your personal goal is to advance to a headship at some point in the future, it is critical that you gain experience in the full range of duties associated with leading a school. You may become expert in addressing parent concerns, but if you are not perceived as competent in budget management, you may find it difficult to convince others that you are ready to serve as a headteacher.

It is absolutely essential, therefore, that you work to develop skills and expertise in as many areas of school management as you can whilst serving as a deputy. It is your task to broaden your portfolio to demonstrate capacity for addressing many different functional areas of operating a school.

How can this happen? The first step should probably involve a frank conversation with your headteacher. It will probably not surprise her or him that you have ambitions to some day lead your own school. Explain what may be quite obvious: you need to gain insights into many different areas of school management and leadership. Your annual performance management review is an ideal opportunity to express your aspirations. Further, it is the time to link these to specific staff development opportunities and targets, as outlined above.

Stay Alive Professionally

If you are now a deputy headteacher, you will no doubt find the observation that you are very busy in your job amusing. Simply keeping your head above water and addressing all of the duties assigned to you is quite a task. But if you want to be a head, you may have to do more. For example, you cannot neglect the need to stay attuned to professional issues, research, and other development in the field of education and educational research. To state the obvious, pursuing a personal professional development agenda is not always consistent with what is listed in your daily diary.

Despite the limitations of time (and energy), two recommendations are made for personal growth while you strive to refine your leadership skills.

One is through reading and the other is by participating in courses, professional seminars and conferences.

Engaging in a reading agenda is a relatively simple activity, although going home to read a book after a hard day at school is not something that you would necessarily place high on a personal priority list. However, if you are going to keep current in professional practice trends and research, the single best way to do so is to keep up with recent literature. You cannot possibly become an expert on everything presented in the literature, but you may carve out an area in which you do most of your reading.

In the space below, indicate any recent books or other material you have read (or plan to read in the near future). Indicate what appeals to you most about this material and your duties as a deputy.

....

....

....

....

....

....

The second recommended practice to help deputy headteachers remain alive professionally involves participation in courses, seminars and conferences. To a large extent, your ability to follow through with this suggestion is dependent on available resources and the goodwill of your headteacher. Simply stated, conferences and other similar activities cost money and time away from your job. On the other hand, even if it might mean using some of your own finances and spending personal time or weekends to attend professional meetings, think about doing so for at least two reasons. First, you are likely to learn some important things about topics that may be important to your work now and in the future. Second, attending professional meetings will put you in contact with many other people who will, in turn, get to know you and your abilities. That form of self-marketing through personal networks will have considerable value when you begin look around for a headship of your own.

Indicate any professional conferences or seminars in which you have recently participated. Indicate some of the benefits you believe you have acquired through your involvement.

....

....

....

....

....

....

What professional events would you like to attend during the next year or two?

....

....

....

....

....

....

The critical thing to remember, regardless of what approaches you may follow, is that if your goal is to grow into a headship some day, then you will need to continue to grow professionally.

Stay Positive

The last recommendation offered to you as a deputy headteacher may be the single most powerful one, because it touches on all the other items listed. Be as positive and enthusiastic as you can about yourself, your job, your colleagues, and most of all, your pupils. That is not always an easy thing to do, of course. As a school leader, a big part of your life automatically involves problems and conflict. It is more than a bit tempting to spend an inordinate amount of time feeling bad about your job. In short, it may be easy to become quite cynical and begin looking for the worst features of life as an educator.

Now, stop and think about what dwelling on problems might do for you as you begin to build your career. Imagine that you are involved with searching for a new headteacher for your school. Also, think what reaction you would probably have to an applicant for that position if he or she spent a good deal of time criticizing or complaining about their present school. Compare your impressions of that person with someone who has a reputation for being positive, enthusiastic and a genuine supporter for their present situation. Given those two alternatives as applicants, if equally qualified for the headship, most schools will select the person who is more positive.

Building an image as someone who is enthusiastic and happy cannot take place only during the few weeks in which you might be an active candidate for a job, of course. A reputation as a team player who can make a positive contribution as a headteacher gets built over a long period of time and as the result of many things. It is critical to remember that you are on stage during your entire career. Whether you know it or not, people are looking at you as a potential candidate for future positions. As soon as it is clear that a headteacher will be retiring or leaving, people begin to think of possible candidates as replacements. You want to be on that list. The way to do that is to be visible and perceived as a person who would be a positive addition to a school.

When you are at meetings with people from other schools, it is critical that you be a supporter of your present school. No matter what others may say or believe about your present situation, your public stance must be one of commitment and support to the best place you can possibly be – at least for now. Taking any other stance creates an image that you do not want, such as fearing what you may do or say about their school if you become their headteacher. People want to believe if you become leader of "our school" you will support them as much as you do in your present position.

* * *

Regardless of any problems that might exist in your present school, list ten or more features of your present situation that make it a good place to work.

....

....

....

....

....

....

....

....

....

....

Make a copy of your list and read it over each time you head out of your door. Do not do a similar listing of problems and shortcomings. Even even if saying these things would not have a negative effect on your career, no one really wants to hear your problems.

Stay positive, be enthusiastic and project an image that allows people to have confidence that you will be the same kind of person in your next job.

Your Personal Plan

If you are currently a deputy headteacher who wishes to become a head in the near future, review the learning strategies suggested in this chapter. Identify those issues that you believe are most relevant to you, and indicate what you plan to do during the next year or two. For example, you might wish to identify a few courses that you would like to take to assist you in staying alive professionally.

....

....

....

....

··

··

Suggested Reading

Kerry, Trevor (2000). *Mastering deputy headship: Acquiring skills for future leadership*. London: Parson Education Limited.

National College for School Leadership website. http://www.ncsl.org Of particular interest are descriptions of the NCSL programme, "Entry to the Headship", and also Headlamp and Performance Management Review procedures.

Tranter, Susan M. (2002). *Diary of a deputy*. London: Routledge/Falmer.

6

Others' Expectations

When Mary Kolshar accepted her current post as the headteacher of Upper Arlington Primary School, she felt a mixture of both confidence and anxiety to an extent that she had never known before in her professional life. She believed that she had enough experience as a teacher, head of numeracy, assistant headteacher, and most recently deputy to appreciate most of the major issues that needed to be addressed in an effective school.

On the other hand, Mary was not totally comfortable with the expectations that others had for her performance. She knew that she wanted to spend a lot of time working with staff to assist them in improving their efforts to help the pupils. That seemed to be a statement that made a lot of sense to those who interviewed her when she applied to Upper Arlington. However last week, when the chief education officer met with all of the headteachers in the authority, Mary heard a somewhat different message about the importance of taking charge of things this term through sharing personal visions and goals with the staff. Mary's recent headteacher and mentor, Norma Galloway, always told her that her most critical job as a new headteacher would be to make certain that the premises of her school were in good order. That was Mrs Galloway's approach to letting Mary know that she had to make certain that the technical details of the headteacher's job were very important.

Mary was truly looking forward to her new life as a headteacher, but she was more than a bit confused about whose voice she would be hearing now that the new school term was about to get underway.

* * *

Mary Kolshar is not the only new headteacher who has been given so much good advice that she did not get any advice at all. Everyone has a different idea about what you should be doing. In the long run, you will have to make decisions as to what should be done and how you should define your job as a headteacher. But it is critical to note that there are likely to be numerous competing definitions and descriptions of that very broad job.

This chapter addresses the issue of competing expectations. Research findings about what different individuals have to say about the most important aspects of your work. In the long run, you will have to be the person who decides what is most critical about your work, but some alternative perspectives that may be of interest to you are also shared.

Critical Skills for New Headteachers: A Survey

Before going any further with this discussion of the kinds of skills that different groups expect of you as a new headteacher, take a moment to respond to the items on the survey in Figure 6.1, the Beginning Headteachers' Critical Skills Inventory. This instrument was developed to provide research data that serves as the basis for this chapter.

Scale 1 (items 1–8) deals with the items associated with the technical duties of headteachers. These tend to be the kinds of job responsibilities that are found in written job descriptions. Scale 2 (items 9–16) deals with issues that are defined as socialization skills, or things that a person needs to know, do, or demonstrate to fit into a new organization. Finally Scale 3 (items 17–24) is composed of items that are self-awareness skills, or items that touch on one's personal ability to know one's own values, attitudes and beliefs as they are related to a professional role.

Figure 6.1 Beginning Headteachers' Critical Skills Inventory

Directions: For each of the following duties associated with the role of headteacher, assess the extent to which each item is critical to your ability to do your job. Use the following scale in responding to each item:

5 = *Extremely important*
4 = *Somewhat important*
3 = *Neutral* (not extremely important or totally unimportant)
2 = *Somewhat unimportant*
1 = *Totally unimportant*

Circle one item

Scale 1
1. How to assess staff.   5 4 3 2 1
2. How to conduct group meetings.   5 4 3 2 1
3. How to design and implement a data-based
   improvement process, including target-setting and
   evaluation.   5 4 3 2 1
4. How to develop and monitor a budget for the school.   5 4 3 2 1
5. How to organize and conduct parent conferences.   5 4 3 2 1
6. How to establish school timetables.   5 4 3 2 1
7. Awareness of school law issues.   5 4 3 2 1
8. How to manage catering, cleaning and clerical staff.   5 4 3 2 1
9. Establishing a positive and cooperative relationship with
   other school leaders in your authority.   5 4 3 2 1

Scale 2
10. How to determine who is what in a school setting.   5 4 3 2 1
11. Knowing how to relate to governors and personnel from
    the local authority.   5 4 3 2 1
12. Knowing where the limits exist within the school and
    balancing that knowledge with one's own professional role.   5 4 3 2 1
13. Knowing how the headship changes family and other
    personal relationships.   5 4 3 2 1
14. Developing interpersonal networking skills that may be
    used with individuals inside and outside the school.   5 4 3 2 1
15. Ability to encourage involvement by all parties in the
    educational system.   5 4 3 2 1
16. Understanding how to develop positive relationships with
    other organizations and agencies located in the school's
    surrounding community.   5 4 3 2 1

Scale 3
17. Demonstrating an awareness of what it means to
    possess organizational power and authority.   5 4 3 2 1
18. Demonstrating an awareness of why one was selected
    for the leadership position in the first place.   5 4 3 2 1

19. Portraying a sense of self-confidence on the job.   5 4 3 2 1
20. Having a vision along with the understanding needed
    to achieve organizational goals.   5 4 3 2 1
21. Demonstrating a desire to make a significant difference
    in the lives of students.   5 4 3 2 1
22. Being aware of one's biases, strengths and weaknesses.   5 4 3 2 1
23. Understanding and seeing that change is ongoing and that
    it results in a continually changing vision of leadership.   5 4 3 2 1
24. Knowing how to assess job responsibilities in terms of the
    real role of the headteacher.   5 4 3 2 1

Scoring: Now add up your scores in the following way:

Scale 1: Items 1–8 = ... divided by 8 = ...

Scale 2: Items 9–16 = ... divided by 8 = ...

Scale 3: Items 17–24= .... divided by 8 = ...

Rank-order your three average scores per scale:

....

....

....

Now that you have computed the New Headteachers' Critical Skills Inventory yourself, you have rank-ordered the three broad areas of technical skills (Scale 1), socialization skills (Scale 2), and self-awareness skills (Scale 3). The next section of this chapter looks at your ratings as they compare with those of other individuals who also participated in this research over the years. You will soon appreciate the fact that there is little absolute consensus as to the "ideal" duties of headteachers.

Other Beginners

If you rank-ordered the three areas from most to least important as follows:

1. Technical skills
2. Socialization skills

3. Self-Awareness skills

you were in line with a majority of other new headteachers. In addition, you were consistent with a high percentage of aspiring heads.

Of the 24 items on the survey, which one(s) do you believe to be most important?

....

....

....

....

Which are the least important?

....

....

....

....

Research has found that new heads and people expressing a desire to become headteachers at some point in the future related item 7, "Awareness of issues related to school law", as the most critical skill to be demonstrated, whereas item 17, "Demonstrating an awareness of what it means to possess organizational power and authority", was viewed as least important.

What might these responses imply to you in terms of the perceptions held by colleagues who were not yet in the role of the headteacher, or who have also recently stepped into their first headship?

Experienced Heads

Of the 24 items on the Beginning Headteachers' Critical Skills Inventory, which do you believe were rated as "most important" by heads with at least three years of experience?

....

....

....

....

Which items from the survey were probably rated as least important by the heads, in your mind?

....

....

....

....

According to headteachers and principals who participated in this research, the most critical skill to be demonstrated by a newcomer was item 10, "How to determine who is what in a school setting". This item was followed closely by item 9, "Establishing a positive and cooperative relationship with other school leaders in your authority". Both of these items were in the cluster related to socialization skills.

According to the same group listed above, the least relevant items that need to be demonstrated by newcomers were item 8, "How to manage catering, cleaning and clerical staff", and item 6, "How to establish school timetables". These items, and most others that were among the lowest-rated issues, were clustered in the technical skills category.

What are some of the reasons why you believe that experienced head-teachers might rank these items as they do?

....

....

....

....

....

....

So What Does This Mean?

The fact that different groups hold different expectations for what school leaders are supposed to do is not a new or astonishing finding. However, the study reported here has provided some important insights into differences that, in turn, are related to finding more effective ways of guiding people through personal career transitions and also providing people with more effective experiences as new headteachers.

The implications of this research on perceptions related to critical skills for new headteachers are clear in the induction programmes that are designed to assist novice school managers. For example, the findings of this study suggest that experienced heads value colleagues' ability to demonstrate greater self-confidence and the ability to fit into the social context of a school. This offers a compelling argument for adopting mentoring schemes for new leaders. Chapter 11 will review this topic in greater detail. Here, it should be noted that mentoring for new headteachers often misses the mark about the real issues facing newcomers. The majority of existing mentoring programmes tend to focus on helping people learn critical technical skills. I do not wish to suggest that learning such skills is unimportant or that beginners always have an immediate grasp of how to do a number of things, even if they have had extensive experience as a deputy. On the other hand, it may be considerably more relevant to support novice heads by investing scarce professional development resources in a programme addressing some issues by suggesting that heads delegate some tasks to experienced secretaries and clerks. Then, too, when people take their first headships after serving as deputies for a number of years, they often have a fairly strong repertoire of technical skills. What beginners do not know is how it feels to be in the apex leadership role in a school.

Mentoring for new headteachers is a desirable activity. However, such a practice works best if it is directed largely at supporting novices in their efforts to increase their skills in the areas of increased socialization and self-awareness. Such mentoring ideally focuses on the needs and feelings of the individual as he or she proceeds during the first year or two of professional service.

The establishment of mentoring relationships will not automatically guide you through a successful first year. Having a mentor will certainly help, but you can do things as an individual as well. Understanding that different groups of people have different expectations of what you are supposed to do is extremely important. At this point in your career, you probably believe that the most difficult tasks for headteachers to perform are to take care of the technical side of the job – maintain the budget and schedule, keep within the law, and so on. These are important things for any headteacher.

However, it is also important to note that your colleagues will expect other attributes. Other headteachers in your authority want good colleagues – people who fit in with them and contribute to the well-being of all the local schools. Governors want people who are confident – who believe they can do the job for which they were hired. The research findings suggest that you will not be viewed by others as very successful if you spend all your time taking care of business in your school. Others expect that you can do the job according to an established job description. They want you to add your own personality and ability to the quality of life in your new school. That may be one of the reasons why a lot of beginning headteachers are shocked to find out that they are not viewed in an extremely positive light, even when they have spent a lot of time in their own schools doing the job they were hired to do.

One additional word of explanation and caution. Although the research found that various groups look differently at the relative importance of skills that need to be demonstrated by beginning headteachers, no individual items or categories (technical, socialization or self-awareness) are totally unimportant. Every item on the survey was viewed as critical. However, when faced with a need to prioritize, different groups find certain items more important than others. Although the information presented here is meant to guide you and give you some notion of how others might look at your job, in large measure how you personally view your job and its various responsibilities and tasks must be a matter for you to define on your own. Once again, it is critical to understand and remain consistent with your own personal and professional platform as a way to guide your choices. More information is provided regarding this important activity in Chapter 8.

Your Personal Plan

This chapter concludes by asking you to incorporate the concepts learned in this chapter into your personal professional portfolio as a way to guide your growth as a successful headteacher. Now that you have had the opportunity to think about the kinds of skills you value, as seen by your responses to the New Headteachers' Critical Skills Inventory and compared with the perceptions of others, where do you believe is the greatest degree of difference between what you value and what experienced headteachers and others value?

....

....

....

....

....

....

In what areas do you find the greatest similarities and overlaps between your assumptions about critical skills and the assumptions of experienced heads and others?

....

....

....

....

....

....

In the space below, note some of the ways in which you plan to address the differences that exist between your perceptions of critical skills and the perceptions of your colleagues.

....

....

....

....

....

....

References

National College for School Leadership website <u>http://www.ncsl.org</u> This
reference will provide you with the latest national job descriptions for
headteachers. Links are also provided to the DfES Pay and Conditons
document which details the formal national generic job specifications for
heads. You may wish to review both sets of descriptions and carry out a
personal assessment of which identified tasks in either set of documents
represent strengths and weaknesses in your own case.

7

Learning the Culture of Your School

Trevor Dandridge was excited on this, his first day as the new headteacher of Bayswater Secondary School. Although he had had nine years of successful experience as a secondary school deputy in a neighbouring community, he had always looked forward to the day when he would have his own school. He wanted to step into a setting where he would have the chance to implement some of the ideas he had for more effective ways to help adolescent learners. He enjoyed a reputation as a very innovative teacher. It was not surprising that he now saw a chance of carrying out a lot of his dreams through his new role as the leader of a school.

Trevor was thinking of the things he wanted to do to change the school's instructional practices as he walked into his office. Of course, he had been in the school before this first day on the job. However, he had looked but he really had not seen much during his past visits. He had been so focused on the things that he planned to do as the new headteacher that he could not recall much about the school's physical environment. It was a bit like the experience that he and his wife had several years before when they bought their house. A few hours after signing the agreement to purchase the property, they knew very little about the details of what they had just purchased. All they knew was that it was their home, and they were happy. Ill-fitting cupboard doors were hidden by their immediate enthusiasm.

Trevor looked around his office and noticed that it was a large enough room with a nice window that looked on the play area for the children. He also noticed two more features of his office that he had not paid attention to on earlier visits. A large bookcase covered one wall. It was filled with books and manuals left by the previous head who had not returned since retiring a few months earlier. Trevor looked at the titles of the material left on the shelves. Virtually all of the reading dealt with classroom management techniques or approaches to pupil discipline.

The second thing that Trevor now discovered was that there was a buzzer mounted on the wall outside of his office. When he asked his secretary its purpose, she told him that the previous headteacher was quite adamant about not being disturbed by anyone while he worked in his office – which represented almost all of his time on most days. As a result, he installed the entrance buzzer for individuals to signal their need to speak with the head about "urgent matters". He had made it quite clear that "urgent" was synonymous with "dire emergency" and that anyone who interrupted his work would be dealt with quite severely.

Trevor made a mental note to box up the books and call the former headteacher that afternoon. He asked the caretaker to take the material out of his office as soon as possible. Second, Trevor told a member of the maintenance staff to disconnect the entry buzzer. He also drafted a memo to all staff indicating that he invited people to simply drop in to his office whenever there was a need – urgent or not. His would be an "open door" style of management. He wanted to focus on instruction, not behavioural management. And he wanted to work *with* his staff, not apart from them.

* * *

Start by describing the headteacher of Bayswater School before Trevor came on board.

....

....

....

....

....

....

Some of the descriptions that emerge about Trevor's predecessor include "reclusive", "severe", "attentive to discipline", or "unwilling to ever leave his office". These might be quite unfair generalizations concerning a person's entire professional career or presence in a school. However, the nature of the books and the ways in which the former headteacher controlled contact with the staff contribute to a perception and an image of past practice.

This points to an important issue that a new headteacher needs to address, namely how to reconcile her or his new ways of addressing the headship with those of the last head. It is important for the newcomer to ask, "What did the staff expect of the last headteacher?" as a way to understand what they now expect. In the case of Trevor Dandridge, what are likely to be some of the expectations that the staff has of a headteacher who steps in after the person who did not welcome visitors to his office?

....

....

....

....

....

....

Once again, it is not possible to say absolutely what images the teachers in this school had of the role of the headteacher. But it looks like many people might have thought that the last person was good because he kept an eye on the "bad boys and girls" so the teachers would not be bothered by that type of problem. The former headteacher appears to have not spent much time out in the school or otherwise relating to the staff. Instead, he stayed in his office and responded to the needs of his teachers by attending to management details and pupil discipline. Teachers could teach effectively because the headteacher took care of all the trouble. And the headteacher seems to have been comfortable in that role. After all, his professional library reflected a serious interest in learning about discipline and behaviour management.

Trevor Dandridge may be in for quite a shock when his teachers discover the headteacher out of his office, in the corridors visiting pupils and staff. "How will the new head be able to do what Mr X used to do?" will be a frequent topic among staff. The next few weeks, or even months, will represent a very difficult transition period in which teachers will need to recognize that the former headteacher is gone and, more important, so is the old image of what a headteacher is supposed to do to assist staff. Trevor could be in for a rough time if he does not appreciate these subtle but very critical issues. I am not advocating the maintenance of the old system and image for no reason other than to make teachers comfortable. Quite the contrary; change is often needed, and the new headteacher has been selected at least in part to bring about that kind of change. But it is critical that a newcomer recognizes what existed in the past, who the heroes were, what have been some of the common legends and history of the school, and celebrates the past and moves cautiously towards the future.

Don't Just Look...See

The school you have just inherited has a lot of important signs that you need to be able to see if you are going to understand the culture, appreciate it, celebrate it and then move on. Trevor Dandridge could have been in for a terrible first year if he had looked at the buzzer and the book titles and not seen what they truly represented. Taking time to see might enable a head to appreciate the culture, history, symbols, and general values and expectations of a community.

What didn't you know about the culture of the school where you now work prior to coming to work there for the first time?

....

....

....

....

....

....

List some of the things that you saw when you first came to your present school and that impressed you as signs of "the way things are around here".

....

....

....

....

....

....

What did you do in response to these things?

....

....

....

....

....

....

Who are some of the heroes of your school? Why are they so important?

....

....

....

....

....

....

When a newcomer first arrives, it is critical that that person spends time looking very carefully at the whole environment to see what story is being told. It is also an important exercise for teachers who think they know their school but who will have a new and different perspective if they return to their school in a different role (i.e. as headteacher or deputy). For example, did the former head arrange his or her desk in a way that it served as a barrier to people who came into the office? Do classrooms give evidence of very formal, lecture-type arrangements? If so, what might these signs suggest about the climate or ethos of the school in which you now work? What do you see in the teachers' rooms? Is there evidence of a great deal of good-natured banter among teachers while in the staff room? If you see your office decorated with your predecessor's belongings, are there any examples of the teachers' relationships with the head? For example, are there such things as gifts or memory books provided to the former headteacher by members of staff?

The critical issue here is that "a school is not a school is not..." Each school, regardless of size, type, location, level of pupils served, geographic site, and just about every other variable selected, has a completely different reality, history and feel about it. Like individual people, schools have different personalities. Often, these personalities are easier to identify than one might assume. If a newcomer takes time to see the subtle signs of the system, rather than quickly glancing at things, the true reality of a school will become apparent.

Do not forget, too, that you need to be able to identify what may be called the "informal organization of your school". This refers to the people and things that do not have formal titles, but influence what goes on in your school each day. Informal leaders in your school, or key influential people, need to be recognized as soon as possible. Also take time to learn about the subcultures in your school. Many people make a huge mistake by walking into a school and assuming that all teachers are one group, secretaries are another, and so on. Factions exist, and loyalties appear from one small group to another. For example, some of your teachers may be ardent supporters of the teachers' unions. Others may belong to the same unions, but are less committed to the agreed goals.

Listen...Don't Just Hear

The importance of seeing a school and not simply looking at it is similar to taking time to listen to what is happening in a school. It is important to remain attentive to the sounds and language of your new environment. They provide many subtle indicators of the ethos and informal organization in which you now work.

Listen carefully to the words teachers use to describe the pupils. Are they filled with warmth and support? Or do they express a constant battle between "us" and "them"? Do the "war stories" shared in the staff room reflect instances of adults controlling children? Or, are the stories shared about successes in achieving positive results? Of course, most schools will have a mixture of both kinds of teacher talk. But in some schools the prevailing philosophy of the teachers in relation to their work with pupils is visible and needs to be recognized (if not necessarily endorsed) by a new headteacher. One of the challenges that a head may face involves changing staff attitudes towards children. But changes cannot take place on the first day, and ignoring past attitudes will not help the change process.

How would you describe the teacher talk about pupils and other issues in your school?

....

....

....

....

....

....

Another important indicator of your new school is what you hear in your office as clerks, secretaries, cafeteria workers, caretakers, or other staff members have contact with pupils, parents, teachers and members of the general public. Any new headteacher would do well to listen attentively to the tone of the language (friendly and cordial or businesslike and cold) that people use with individuals from outside the school. Have you ever telephoned a business and then decided to go elsewhere because of the way you were addressed? People experience the same feelings when they call a school.

If you knew nothing about your school other than the sound of your secretary's voice, what impressions would you have of your school?

....

....

....

....

....

....

Another thing that listening to subtle sounds in your school will tell you is the degree of formality that exists in the school in which you have recently become the headteacher. Do teachers call you by your surname immediately? It is not unusual to hear teachers who have worked together for many years continue to use formal terms when addressing each other, at least during the school day. Respect that tradition; calling Mrs Johnson

"Sue" in front of her pupils may be offensive and may distance you from a teacher who might otherwise become one of your strongest allies.

Walk through the corridors of your school and listen to the sounds you hear, the sounds coming out of classrooms. Is there a lot of good-natured laughing or a considerable amount of raised voices indicating that teachers are disciplining pupils? Or is it extremely quiet? Any of these signs may be indicative of the general tone of your school.

If a person who knew little about your school walked through the school one day and listened, what kind of impressions would he or she take away?

....

....

....

....

....

....

Celebrate the Past

A natural, unavoidable contradiction exists when a new headteacher walks into a school. On one hand, the new leader is expected to do something, bring about change of some sort, and make a difference. You might call this a type of "Hit them hard and hit them early" approach to change. Some favour this style because a new leader always has a bit of a "honeymoon period" that allows changes to be made without too much fuss. This is true whether the former headteacher was viewed as extremely positive or as ineffective. People expect a newcomer to represent a new order of things. On the other hand, schools are very fragile and normally very conservative organizations. "The way we have always done things" is a strong force that people seek to maintain. Thus, the new headteacher might be criticized for not doing enough but also doing too much at the same time.

Consider the dilemma facing Trevor Dandridge. He knew that he had been hired to be an instructional leader, but he noticed that his predecessor had been primarily an office-bound disciplinarian. If he did not bring about change and assert himself in one way, he would not be fulfilling the promises he made while being selected for the post. On the other hand, when he proclaimed that he would no longer serve as the school's primary disciplinarian and remain in his office, some teachers were upset. What was he to do?

The fictional Trevor Dandridge is patterned on a headteacher who now has more than ten years of experience. He is respected by his teachers and his site-based council. However, if someone could invent a magical instrument called a "retrospectoscope" to look back in time, it might be possible to second-guess decisions made by Trevor at the beginning of his headship so that he could have had a smoother start.

Perhaps the most significant thing that Trevor did to make his start a bit more troublesome was that he did not talk to any of his new staff members about their perceptions of why the former headteacher did some of the things he did. Trevor had the right to change the image of the headship from one of isolated chief disciplinarian to instructional leader. In fact, his efforts ought to be commended. But when he took steps to remove any sign of his predecessor from the school, he was symbolically denying something that many of his teachers probably did not feel comfortable about losing. Even if many of the teachers did not like the former headteacher, Trevor's actions seemed to suggest that the teachers and former head were wrong. At the very least, it was very important for Trevor to share what he planned to do with several staff members. He could have assured them that he was not going to discredit the fine work of the past. Rather, he was simply trying to start things off with a different perspective of someone new to the school.

Another thing that Trevor could have done shortly after the beginning of the new school term was to invite the former headteacher to visit his old school and talk with Trevor about some of his visions of the school. In addition, some discussions about the history, culture, and traditions of the school could help both the new and former heads develop insights regarding the school, staff and pupils.

Do you have any additional suggestions for how the shift from one headteacher to the next could be made less traumatic?

....

....

....

....

....

....

It is critical that new headteachers do not charge into their new settings so forcefully that they do not give honour to the past. Former members of staff, practices, policies and traditions might need to be replaced, but they need to be publicly respected because they represent many subtle signs of life in an organization. Any newly arrived leader who does not celebrate the good work of the past may have many unnecessary battles with people who might see the newcomer as unfeeling or insensitive to the local culture. By the same token, remember that one of the things a new leader needs to do is assess the practices of the past and determine what was viewed negatively by parents, staff and others. Simply wanting to avoid the appearance of getting rid of all past practices does not mean that you must be bound to repeat undesirable work as well.

Developing an Action Plan

Describe the most important aspects of the school culture that you inherited as the new headteacher, that is, the kinds of things you must understand as you step in as the new leader.

Which elements of the past culture represent things you cannot comfortably live with as the new headteacher?

....

....

....

....

....

....

What practices appear to have been least popular with staff, pupils and parents?

....

....

....

....

....

....

How do you plan to keep away from these past practices in a way that will not alienate you from your staff or other important people in your school environment?

....

....

....

....

....

....

How do you hope to replace the things that you are not comfortable with in your new school? Why?

....

....

....

....

....

....

What are some of the features of your new school you believe should be maintained as much as possible? Why?

....

....

....

....

....

....

8

Reviewing Personal Values

New headteachers experience difficulties during their first years on the job for many reasons. In some cases, they do not take care of business. For example, they might ignore the importance of completing tasks on time, or they might violate policies or laws. Another reason for people getting into trouble is that they do not seem to have the kind of people skills needed to communicate effectively with others.

In this chapter, the focus is on yet another area found to be a serious problem for many new school leaders. Research on new leaders' problems identifies the importance of people coming to grips with their own set of personal values and priorities as they engage in the activities required of headteachers.

Case Study: Because It's Important to Me

Charles Davis, headteacher at Fuller Point Secondary School, was in trouble. For the fourth month in a row, he had failed to provide his governors with data concerning the strategies that were planned for implementation in response to the low scores that were attained in last year's GCSE exams at the school. The low place in the national league tables was enough to cause his predecessor to retire earlier than expected. One of the things that Charles had promised when he was interviewed for the headship was to "turn things around". The governors wanted to see progress, and so they were keen to see what things were being done each month during this critical turn-around year. Charles had promised a detailed written report each month, but after the first of these statements that was presented in October, no further updates had been provided. The governors were growing weary of what they perceived to be predicted excuses at each meeting. Was Charles stalling, or was he simply inept?

From Charles's perspective, developing detailed monthly reports of progress to present to the governors was far from his highest priority. After all, he had taken over a school filled with many problems. It was nearly placed on a programme of special measures last year by the LEA for its failure to hit several achievement targets during the last three years. Charles found a group of experienced but uninvolved teachers who had apparently simply given up. They frequently blamed their inability to teach on the belief that the students, mostly working class children from the homes of recent immigrants, were simply unable or unwilling to work at school. As a result of this pervasive attitude, Charles had spent most of his time in school each day talking to teachers, carrying out in-service sessions, and visiting the homes of many pupils to learn about family issues that may have had an impact on learning. In short, Charles was not as interested in preparing reports. His decision was to spend the bulk of his time and energy determining root causes. After that, he would gladly begin to describe action plans. But at this point, he did not know what actions would be appropriate.

* * *

Headteachers make hundreds of decisions every day. Each is made through certain lenses that the individual brings to the job. And the sources of these lenses are varied. Some come from written policies and laws. These are relatively easy decisions to make. However, headteachers are called upon each day to make other decisions that are not easily defined because they are not based on policy or law.

Consider, for example, decisions such as the one Charles Davis had to make in the case above. Charles had to decide whether or not he would comply with the expectations of his governors, or if he would use his time in other ways. What is the deciding factor? Charles's personal and professional values have a lot to do with his ultimate choice (and also the probable consequences resulting from his decisions). Charles Davis valued contact with his teachers and pupils more than he did preparing a report. No policy guided his decision.

Most decisions made by headteachers are matters of personal choice. In many cases, the reasons headteachers use for making their decisions are unclear to the outside observer. Mrs Jones gets to take her children to the museum, but Mr Smith is not permitted to go. Teachers complain about the apparent lack of consistent behaviour of the head. Yet headteachers often do not seem concerned about what others believe are inconsistent patterns of behaviour. However, experienced principals have learned – often the hard way – that differences in perceptions, whether they are right or wrong, represent real beliefs and views of others. As a consequence, these perceptions must be understood, appreciated and addressed.

Chapter 2 discussed the importance of developing a strong sense of self-awareness as a critical skill for new headteachers. Remember that of all the attributes noted, the most valued was the ability to show clearly one's personal beliefs and values and a recognition of why one was selected for a leadership role in the first place.

Self-awareness about one's duties and responsibilities in a job comes about largely as the product of a reflective process in which one constantly matches the requirements of the job with a personal value system. The more a person is content that his or her choice of a career is consistent with the most important attitudes, beliefs and values that drive a person, the more satisfied he or she will be – and the more effective, productive and ultimately successful. It is a simple fact that when a person becomes more invested in a job as a personal commitment, he or she will not only be more satisfied but more effective as well.

The strategy that I'm suggesting as a way to review one's personal value and belief system as it relates to the realities of the job of the headship is by a periodic review of something called a personal educational platform. A platform is a philosophical statement, although I avoid the term "philosophical" because many practitioners stay away from such airy tasks. A platform statement puts into writing some of the dearest beliefs that a person might have about the educational issues that define a major part of his or her work life. It is often said that the major planks in a platform express an individual's non-negotiable values. In many ways, they represent the core values of a person – the kinds of things that, if violated by the nature of the job one has to do or other factors, would cause a person to leave. A personal educational platform has the power of putting on paper the bottom line of an individual educator.

Finally, a statement of a platform has the potential either (a) to guide a person away from a professional role that is inconsistent with personal values, or (b) to enable a person to know when a particular placement in a job is not what was envisioned in the first place. For example, a platform can help a person recognize that selecting headship as a career goal was a good choice or if taking a particular headship in a specific community was the best move. In either case, if the personal values that are expressed in a platform are not attainable in a job in one location, it may be reasonable to move on.

Building a Platform

In the pages that follow, I will lead you through the development of an educational platform. Many different approaches might be followed in carrying out this exercise. You are invited to modify anything offered here so that it is more consistent with your own needs, interests, and of course, personal values.

You will be asked several questions that have to do with the central issues faced by educators. After each question, space is provided for you to write down your responses. Simply filling in the blanks does not necessarily mean that you have prepared an educational platform. However, your answers might serve as an appropriate foundation for a more cohesive statement that you will craft in the future.

1. What is my view of the purpose of schooling?

People have struggled with this issue for almost as long as formal schooling has existed. Is it your view that pupils attend schools to acquire skills needed to enter immediately into the world of work? For moral development? For a foundation in tertiary education? Perhaps for other purposes, as noted below.

....

....

....

....

....

....

2. What are the key ingredients of an "adequate education" for all pupils?

There has been a lot of talk about what the focus of schools should be. Each educator must have some sense of what the basic elements of good schooling might include.

....

....

....

....

....

....

3. What is the appropriate role for pupils?

Perhaps an even more important issue to be considered here concerns one's personal view of who pupils are. It is widely assumed that educators all have a core value that speaks to the centrality of the needs of pupils as the driving force in schools. Although this may sound appealing and "right", is it truly your vision and value?

....

....

....

....

....

....

4. What is the appropriate role for teachers?

Again, the question might revolve around your personal definition of who teachers are in the first place. Some people might view teachers as true professionals who have the best interests of their pupils in mind as they proceed with their duties. Others view teachers as employees who can be easily replaced with others when the need arises. Are these views consistent with your perspective, or do you have other notions of who teachers are and what they should be doing in schools?

....

....

....

....

....

....

5. What is the appropriate role for parents and other community members?

Do you feel that parents are truly partners in the educational programme of your school, or are they intruders? What about your views of other community members? What is the preferred relationship between your school and local businesses?

....

....

....

....

....

....

6. What is my personal definition of "curriculum"?

Modern definitions of effective headteachers note that they are instructional leaders. What does this mean in practice? In the UK, how does the National Curriculum affect the ways in which you can serve as a leader in your school?

....

....

....

....

....

....

7. *What do I want this school to become?*

What is your personal vision for the school? What kinds of hopes and dreams for a more effective school drive your work? What are your ideals?

....

....

....

....

....

....

8. *How to know if students have truly learned?*

The ultimate goal of any school must be to ensure that learning has taken place among students. But what are the indicators, at least in your mind, of whether or not this has really taken place?

....

....

....

....

....

....

9. *How do I want others to see me?*

It is important for leaders to reflect on the kinds of images that they wish to project to followers. How do you hope that you will be viewed by your teachers, pupils and community members? Think about this issue in two ways, as a headteacher and as a person.

....

....

....

....

....

....

10. *What are my non-negotiable values?*

This last question might be the single most important issue to be addressed in your platform. Ultimately, this question asks you to consider the kinds of things that, if violated, would cause you to throw your keys on the table and seek employment elsewhere.

....

....

....

....

....

....

What Do You Do With the Platform?

The value in an educational platform is not found by simply writing it out once, putting it in a drawer and then letting it sit there for the remainder of your professional life. Rather, it should be seen as a living document regarding the parameters that you will put around decisions made during your career. Platforms will change as you move through your professional life. For example, your thinking about how national testing will serve to measure pupil growth and progress may change drastically from day to day until some point in the future. Your vision of "perfect" teachers may be modified greatly as you move further in to your managerial role.

The development of a formal statement of values through the educational platform has many important applications that can be of great assistance to you as you travel through your career as an educational leader. For one thing, developing clarity regarding your non-negotiable values – even though these might change in the future – can be a genuine help to you as you think about changes of positions, moving to other schools and so on. Perhaps being able to stay at home more with your family, or being closer to parents, is something that will need attention in the future.

Second, the articulation of a clear statement of an educational platform is of value to those with whom you are to work. It is not a good idea to print multiple photocopies of your platform and then send them around to everyone you might meet! However, people who have taken the time to write their platforms from time to time inevitably have a stronger grasp of their own values, so that those around them are able to see what makes them tick. This not only has the benefit of enabling heads to be open to their staff, but is also a powerful way to model communication skills that lead to more effective schooling in general. In the long run, becoming clearer about your personal educational values will assist you when you seek other professional positions. For example, an opening for a headship in another school might not be nearly as desirable once you consider the possible compromises that might be needed with regard to your personal values.

Finally, the ultimate value of developing a clear statement of an educational platform may be that it can serve as the foundation for long-term professional development. Too often educators simply drift through their careers and engage in sporadic and periodic programmes of professional development based on learning about one topic or another. In many cases, headteachers simply respond to the visions or platforms of others. It would be far more desirable for headteachers to engage in systematic career planning that is rooted in their own values and in a sense of where they are going or what is important to them. For this reason, it is often suggested that people begin their professional development portfolios with a clear statement of their platforms. In that way, other elements of the portfolio are able to flow in a logical sequence from a strong foundation.

Your Personal Plan

In the next few pages, sketch out some of the more critical elements of your personal portfolio and growth plan. You may wish to consult and respond to the questions posed earlier, or you may respond to other critical issues that will provide a greater sense of who you are as a professional educator.

....

....

....

....

....

....

Now that you have written the planks of your platform, the last step in this self-improvement process involves a clear statement of what you plan to do to implement your personal vision of effective practice. Once you have completed this last step, a final valuable activity involves sharing your statement with one or two close friends, family members, or colleagues with a request that they indicate whether or not they recognize in you some of what you have written and whether or not you have written a real or ideal description.

....

....

....

....

....

....

....

....

....

....

9

Being a Leader

Sharon Mitchell was excited when she received word that she had been selected as the new headteacher of O'Hare Primary School, a small school with a reputation for dedicated and effective teachers and very supportive parents. While serving as the deputy at Logan Primary, near to O'Hare, she was always impressed with the place and she was now extremely pleased that her first headship would be at such a fine school.

Soon after she moved into her new school, Sharon began to realize that being a headteacher carried a lot of responsibility not generally covered in her official job description. She saw that none of her earlier experiences had completely prepared her for the day when she stood alone in her office as the new leader.

She quickly understood that now that she was a headteacher, people reacted to her quite differently. She had known many of the teachers at O'Hare for many years. But now, as they were returning to the school for the new term, Sharon felt a bit of a chill in their attitudes towards her. She was no longer the colleague they had interacted with in the past. Also, it now seemed like a major production just to get out of her school at the same time each day so that she could get home to prepare her family's dinner, a task that she looked forward to simply because it reminded her of a time when she could really get something accomplished in a predictable fashion.

Another reality that Sharon began to appreciate was the fact that, despite being surrounded by a great many different people each day, she felt increasingly as if she were isolated from contact with others. She recalled hearing this in the past from heads with whom she had worked. She first believed that she would be able to combat this feeling by developing a collegial relationship with her Chair of Governors, but this soon became an impractical strategy. After all, it was difficult to confide in the Chair because he would be the person most influential in the Performance Management

Review that would be carried out later that year. Further, the Chair seemed to be a nice enough person, but he had little in common with Sharon. He was a local businessman, and Sharon had spent most of her adult life working in schools.

Finally, Sharon was becoming increasingly weary of the seemingly endless parade of parents and other community members who came to her door on a daily basis with "just one more simple little question" or request, often issues that had been denied by her predecessor. But Sharon was new on the scene, and many people wanted to test her resolve about a variety of issues.

* * *

When people take their first headships, the reactions and situations are often not very different from the scenario described above. Being named as a headteacher may be the fulfilment of a lifelong ambition. All the conditions associated with a particular position might be quite favourable in terms of the location of a school, the individual's feelings of comfort with a school, the reputation of the teachers and so on. Even with all of these factors going the right way, however, it is impossible to ignore the fact that when you become a head the first time, you will face certain issues. One of these is that people will look at you differently, expect different things from you, and hold you accountable in ways that will be markedly different from what they did in the past. Simply stated, you are now the leader and this designation carries certain challenges and demands. Once again, this fact reinforces the demand described in earlier chapters, namely that a critical skill for beginners must be recognition of how the job of being a head-teacher is related to your own sense of self.

No matter how well prepared you may feel as you move into a formal leadership role for the first time, it is impossible to escape the fact that being the boss brings with it certain pressures and demands. This chapter will identify some of the things that any newcomer is likely to face during the first part of the transition into the headteacher's office. If you have served a lengthy term in the capacity of a deputy, you have no doubt had some insights into these issues, although there is still no substitute for serving as the top leader of a school. When the weight of full responsibility for an organization falls on your shoulders, it is very different from serving as a deputy.

This chapter also includes some practical hints for helping you to increase your self-awareness and feelings of identity so that you can meet the pressures of leadership with greater confidence.

Others' Perceptions

As Sharon Mitchell discovered very quickly, one of the things that changes almost immediately when you become a headteacher is the way other people see you. Of course, you are not likely to feel markedly different from the way you did just before becoming a head. Admittedly you are now likely to be more fatigued, and you no doubt feel as if there are not enough hours in a day to carry out your new job. But down deep, you know that you are still the same person you have been for your whole life. It is just that people around you – teachers, office staff, parents, and pupils – suddenly perceive you differently and interact differently with you. You should not deliberately try to change, but you need to recognize that the perceptions of others can be powerful forces that will affect you directly or will affect the ways in which other people will see you. In the long run, these are the kinds of things that will enable you to be more effective as a headteacher.

Before I list some of the ways beginners are perceived differently by people who work with them, if you are currently in your first year as a headteacher list some of the ways you have noticed people treating you differently from how they did in the past.

....

....

....

....

....

....

Researchers have noted that new leaders receive signals from teachers, fellow heads, parents, community members, pupils and even immediate family members that suggest that they are somehow different now from how they were in the past.

Teachers still tend to look towards someone being in charge. As a result, the role of the formal school leader may change somewhat in tone (from "director" to "facilitator"). But when you are a headteacher, people will continue to look at you as a person who will make critical decisions in times of need. What is often difficult to remember, however, is that each teacher has a very strong sense of when the time of need arises. Some staff members will rarely come directly to you as the headteacher to make decisions for them. On the other hand, every school will have a teacher or two (or more) who will rely on you as the leader to tell them what should be done about even seemingly insignificant issues.

A second aspect of becoming a leader relates to the notion that the headteacher is truly "in the hot seat". When you are in charge of something, whether it is a small primary school or a large secondary school, you are the person who is ultimately responsible for the effective operation of that organization. You cannot make a mistake and then blame it on someone else. Having made that last statement, however, there are nonetheless some headteachers who attribute any unpopular decision made to the fact that "the Council made me do it", or "we have to do it because of the governors". Such heads are often not respected by their peers, and they are usually not terribly effective leaders.

Another price paid by novices is often the loneliness they suddenly feel in their schools and authorities. It is ironic that, in many cases, individuals move into leadership positions because they are recognized as people with great interpersonal and social skills, leading many to believe that they will carry these skills with them into the headteacher's office. Many newcomers to the headship are not surprised to discover that they have crossed the line from teaching to leadership and management. After all, they have served in a number of management roles in schools over the years. This conditioned them to appreciate that they were no longer attached to their colleagues in classrooms. But the final step into the headteacher role has the effect of distancing an individual beyond other levels. Now, when the headteacher walks into the staff room, people look at him or her, nod politely, but separate from the person now perceived as "different" and as a leader/manager.

So What Do You Do?

People start to look at you very differently when you take on the role of the headteacher. They react to this in a number of ways, some of which may be quite unproductive. For example, some new headteachers discover that their staff is not engaging them in the ways they did in the past. The head's reaction may be to put the staff out of their life. They begin to build walls and isolate themselves. Soon, headteachers who adopt this stance begin to spend most of their time in their offices or away from their schools. A common symptom of this situation involves the head beginning to view things in terms of "us" (or "me") versus "them".

Another behaviour often adopted by headteachers who sense separation from their staff is the tendency to internalize everything and make everything their sole responsibility. They stop delegating even small tasks. The result can be very unfortunate as these headteachers feel stress increasing because they do not have time to do everything, they have no friends, they cannot rely on anyone, they have no one to help them do their jobs, and so on.

A third approach seen in some new headteachers faced with the sense that they are no longer accepted by their teaching colleagues is to be deliberately officious. They hide behind rules, regulations, policies, procedures and anything else that might depersonalize their jobs. In this way, they can develop their sense that they are not involved with people who are rejecting them. Their stance is one of coming to work, following rules, avoiding conflict whenever possible, and then going home without worrying about the people with whom they work. Unsurprisingly they tend not to be very happy people at work.

Finally, some new headteachers deal with their sense of separation from staff by rejecting their duties and striving to appear still part of the teaching team, even though the days of the teaching head in most schools are over. Some major problems will arise when new heads avoid becoming a leader. It is important to remember, for example, that headteachers are ultimately responsible for assessing staff. Clearly, heads should not avoid contact with staff simply because of this evaluative function.

The fact is, no matter how you may wish to deal with it, the step you have taken from your former life as a classroom teacher means that certain relationships will change and that new expectations and demands will naturally follow you into your new role. But that sort of transition does not have to be traumatic or cause the kind of negative behaviour I have noted above. The trick of management is to demonstrate your caring about others through the establishment of trust. When you achieve that level of interaction, differences between you, the leader, and the staff will begin to disappear. In short, if you want separation, you can find it. On the other hand, if you want effective teamwork, you have to work on that too, but it can be achieved.

Being in charge of any organization can be stressful and can serve to make a person feel alone and even rejected by others from time to time. This is particularly true in those cases in which people are promoted from within – one day they work with a group of people, but the next day they are making those same people work for them. Things can be done to reduce the sense of separation one feels and without resorting to ways described above. Your job is not to agonize over the sense of separation but to promote a sense of unity in your school.

What are some of the ways in which you have addressed the issue of feeling apart from your teachers now that you have "crossed the line" and become the boss? (For example, some headteachers promote periodic "sharing sessions" in which they invite staff to spend an hour talking about professional concerns they are facing.)

....

....

....

....

....

....

Strategies to Reduce Isolation

The best way to help you reduce your sense of becoming isolated involves making links with key people inside and outside your school.

Inside your school, it is critical that you build bridges with a few key individuals who can serve as sounding boards for you throughout the school year. This is not always an easy task. It is nearly impossible to tell who can be trusted as a confidant when you first walk into a new school. Nevertheless, it is essential to find allies in your immediate environment. The first person who might come to your mind as a person to be trusted is your secretary. He or she will probably know more about the real issues that face your school than just about anyone else you will first encounter. The only thing that needs to be safeguarded in such situations, of course, is the possibility that insights into what and who are important in your new school might be clouded by that other person's perceptions. Also, there is a possibility that well-intentioned conversations about key people in your school might become opportunities for hearsay and gossip. Secretaries have great insights into what is going on in schools. On the other hand, at times they do not know all the reasons why people behave in the ways they do.

Another absolutely critical source of information is your deputy, a person who has probably served at your school for quite a while before you arrived. The same is true of all the other members of the senior management team that you have inherited. A caution exists with regard to this recommendation, however. It is important to recall that others in the school probably have personal agendas that are more important to them than necessarily providing you with accurate information as the incoming head. Despite this reservation, however, reliance on deputies and other members of existing management teams as sources of important information about your new school can effectively reduce your sense of isolation from what is really going on.

A third source of potential support inside your school may be teachers with whom you can feel comfortable in opening up and sharing some personal concerns. These people may not be visible at first as you move into a school; you will have to spend time and make an effort to find teachers who can be trusted on a continuing basis. Remember, too, that those who come forward in the first few days of your new managerial role are often the last people who will become enduring supporters. In this regard, you should rely on experiences that you had in the past. You learned about finding trustworthy allies when you were a deputy, or when you had other key management roles in schools. You also learned about locating allies when you were in a classroom. This process of locating key and trustworthy individuals becomes yet another example of how your platform is an important resource. How do you look at teachers, for example? As you think through your responses to this question, it is likely that your relationships with a few valued colleagues will emerge.

Finally, as you try to assess key issues and other key aspects of the internal realities of your school, do not forget that in many cases you will have inherited a structure for operating your school that may be quite helpful. It is likely that committees and task forces that were formed prior to your arrival are already in place. Spending time with members of these groups can be an important tool for you as you try to develop a comprehensive and positive picture of the culture and operations of your new school.

As you think about your present school, who might be included in your inner circle of confidants?

....

....

....

....

....

....

Your Personal Plan

The issues reviewed in this chapter deal with self-awareness or role awareness skills as one of the concerns of beginning headteachers. In the space below, you may wish to write down some of your frustrations that you are now experiencing because you are the leader in your school. These frustrations may be linked to the items identified earlier, or they might be unique concerns that you have found relate to your first job as a headteacher. In either case, you ought to include these issues as part of building your own personal portfolio and growth plan. Unless you identify some of those issues, you will never be able to deal effectively with them. For each item listed as a frustration, you may also indicate some of the ways in which you have been able to cope with it and proceed with your work as an educational leader.

....

....

....

....

....

....

10

Building a Personal Timetable for Learning and Development

Barbara Phillips was determined not to make the same mistakes that others had made when they first became headteachers. She knew that other novices had stepped into their jobs with the clear intention of "surviving" their first year by sitting back and waiting for things to happen. Barbara believed that as a new headteacher of a very formal and traditional school, she had only a brief "honeymoon period" – a window of opportunity in which she could make the kinds of changes that would enable her school to become more effective. She was committed to hitting the ground running and pushing hard for reforms in her school.

Barbara was also aware of the fact that as a new headteacher, she had much to learn about her school. She was beginning to recognize that she might be burned out before the start of the next term.

* * *

Often, when people achieve a major professional goal such as being appointed as a headteacher for the first time, they have an understandable tendency to want to accomplish a huge amount in as short a time as possible. Indeed, some research even suggests that when people step into a new leadership role, they have only 12 to 18 months to change the organization in which they now work. If they wait too long, there is a strong tendency for them to become a part of the existing scenery, part of the organization that should be changed. This finding, incidentally, is contrary to conventional wisdom that suggests that the new leader should keep a low profile when first coming on board, that he or she should not do anything to upset people by trying to make too many changes too quickly. The problem, of course, is that moving too fast as a new leader has serious drawbacks. Changes might occur, but the cost to the new person might be more than is reasonable as health begins to fail, personal relationships suffer, and followers get caught up in a hectic pace that cannot be maintained for very long.

As new headteachers review their personal values, disposition for leadership, and actual leadership skills, they will need to develop a plan and a related timetable to guide their personal and professional development as teachers. This planning process is the focus of this chapter.

A central tenet of this book is that simply being equipped with a collection of survival skills to get you through the first year or two on the job is not enough to ensure success. Of course, when you take any new job you have a natural interest in learning how to increase your initial comfort by completing assigned tasks in a competent, timely and efficient manner. There is truth in the old saying that you cannot be a leader if you get sacked. As a result, the emphasis in this book is on what to expect at the start of your career. But avoid the temptation of believing that being "good enough" is an adequate way to look at your career as a headteacher. My goal is to assist you in developing a long-term vision of leadership that goes well beyond simple survival skills.

This chapter will assist you in setting up a personal guideline that you might follow as you journey from being a true novice to eventual status as a veteran educational leader in your present school.

A Developmental Framework

One point needs to be recognized very quickly. As a beginner, you want to do a good job, and the job that you have selected as a career is a big one. There may be a strong tendency for you to want to do a lot of things right away and make certain that everything that you do is a resounding success. After all, the governor board that hired you probably told you on numerous occasions that they were pleased you were joining them, that they had high hopes for you to really "make a diference", and that you were just the right person to do a great job. Perhaps the exact words were not exactly these, but there is little doubt that when a new headteacher comes to a school people have high hopes that the newcomer will either do the same wonderful things accomplished by his or her predecessor or make the kinds of changes that will immediately straighten up the mess left by the previous head. Variations on these two themes are possible, but the fact is that people want the new headteacher to do all sorts of things, beginning from the first days on the job.

As a newcomer you will have a natural tendency to try to please everyone, meet all expectations and do a truly outstanding job at all times. But here is a secret: you cannot do all of the above. Furthermore, if you try to do everything with equal zeal and attention right away, you are likely to be less effective in your new job. Many researchers suggest that people proceed through clearly identified phases as they move into new roles. Here are five suggested phases to consider.

Phase 1

This may be referred to as "coming on board". This period normally lasts one or two years. It begins with a person first being appointed to a headship. It ends at different times for different people, but generally it will be at the point where a person feels comfortable enough with a new role that he or she is no longer concerned about losing a job for failing to do certain assigned tasks. People who are in this phase tend to be mostly concerned about their own survival needs. As a result, discussions about long-term goals and projects for a school are not extremely relevant. Furthermore, a principal in this coming on board phase is likely to think more about his or her personal needs above any concerns related to the professional well-being of his or her staff.

Phase 2

After headteachers have developed some degree of comfort in the job and they are no longer experiencing any serious anxiety about whether or not they are going to survive and simply do the job, they are likely to begin a second developmental phase. At about two years into the job, people should start to seek new ways of measuring effectiveness and success. This phase is called the "searching for success" time, because headteachers at this point in their careers realize that they can do the job, but now they wish to do the job well. This phase is a progression beyond coming on board (Phase 1), but it is a time when heads will still likely be more concerned with their own needs – or personal definitions of success – than they are with the broader needs of colleagues or the total organization. On the other hand, during this phase there should be a definite shift from thinking only about survival as a reactive process to trying to move the school forward proactively. Again, no absolute timetable is established for this phase, but it is normally relatively brief for most people, lasting for only one or two years.

Phase 3
This is a time of "looking outward". It is at this point that many headteachers start to question whether what they are doing is starting to have any positive effect on others. In some ways, it is very difficult to distinguish this stage from Phase 2, because during both phases headteachers tend to focus on the issue of impact of leadership behaviour. The critical issue here, however, is that headteachers at this point are asking the questions "Does what I do really have any effect on the staff, and most importantly, pupils?" and "Can I have a substantive impact on practices here so that we can truly improve this school?" One of the critical things to remember about this phase, if a headteacher enters it, is that the beginning of the phase may not happen until after three or four years of service. On the other hand, some headteachers may spend many years in their jobs without ever entering this phase. But in the case of good headteachers, it is also a phase that will never end.

Phase 4
This stage in a headteacher's career, which may come after about ten years on the job, may be referred to as the "torch-passing" phase. What happens in this phase is the beginning of an interest in trying to find, recruit and prepare other people to take an interest in moving into careers as educational leaders. This is played out by headteachers: (a) taking great pride in selecting specific individuals as members of the management team of the school; (b) encouraging and sponsoring one or more teachers to think about future careers in school management; (c) taking on the duties of sponsorship and, to some extent, mentorship to draw new people into the profession; and (d) taking on their personal duties of developing the talents of others and then improving the profession in general. Clearly, this phase is characterized largely by attention directed towards the needs of others, the school and the profession of the headship in general. It is a significant departure from the first two phases, in which concerns and interests are directed inward. No defined period of time is associated with people moving into this career phase. It may occur after five years of being a head, or after 15 or more years. In some cases it may never be a part of a headteacher's career.

Phase 5

At this point in an individual's career there is a distinct return to personal needs and agendas. Here, attention is focused on the the process of "completing a career". This might appear as getting ready for retirement, or at least some shift into a career that is not the headship. For instance, individuals get to a point where their interests are directed towards other professional opportunities. When a person gets to this point, she or he has more interest in other issues outside the daily responsibilities of the headship.

A few summary observations are in order related to this listing of different developmental phases. First, these five stages are not static or linear. In other words, people might move back and forth from one phase to another. For example, an individual who leaves one headship to take another might go from Phase 3 (looking outward) or even Phase 4 (torch passing) and return to Phase 2 (searching for success) when faced with learning about the norms, expectations and cultures of new schools. In fact, the only phases in this model that are found at relatively predictable points in a career are Phase 1 (coming on board) at the beginning and Phase 5 (completing a career) at the end.

The second observation about the five phases is that not everyone proceeds through all steps. For example, some people never become interested in passing the torch (Phase 4) or even looking outward (Phase 3). They tend to remain interested mostly in their own career needs, with little concern for colleagues or even the schools around them. Although it may be unfortunate, it is nevertheless a reality that people sometimes become so focused on their own situations that they forget about their professional relationships with others. If often happens in personal relationships. Some people also have spent a large part of their careers in the coming on board phase (Phase 1); they never seem to learn to go beyond the limitations and perspectives of novices. Suddenly, they shift from concerns, interests and behaviour associated with newcomers to thinking about completing a career (Phase 5). These headteachers go through an entire career without getting out of the starting block. People probably do not intend to do this, but it is a pattern that can happen if one focuses too early and too quickly on simply serving as a headteacher.

One final observation about the phases is that none of these stages is bounded by any strict time limits. For example, some people proceed quickly through the first three phases, often within the first two or three years of their professional lives. They spend the majority of their careers consciously serving as mentors to other practising or aspiring educational leaders. Some people have even moved rapidly to the completing of a career phase (Phase 5), because their goal in becoming a headteacher in the first place was to use it as a stepping stone to some other career.

You can no doubt think of examples of individual headteachers who were in one or another of these phases. You may also wish to list some examples of what you have already encountered at one or more phases identified here:

....

....

....

....

....

....

What Does This Have to Do With Me?

These phases may be of interest to those concerned with looking at and analyzing the long-term career paths of school leaders. But what relevance do they have for someone like you, who is either getting ready to step into a headship for the first time or going through the first year or two on the job? After all, does it make any sense to think about serving as a mentor some day in the future while you are still trying to find a colleague to help you now?

Unless you realize and look at how careers progress in total, you may be frustrated and limited as you start your life as a headteacher. Typically, individuals walk into LEAs where colleague headteachers may be distributed across all the phases, with one exception: it is not unusual for a person to be the only head who is coming on board (Phase 1) at a single time. As a result, a person can get lost in an environment where everyone else is either thinking about retirement or at least focused almost exclusively on searchving for success (Phase 2) as a personal concern. Any newly hired headteacher needs to find a mentor; however, some LEAs have no heads who are even remotely interested in torch passing (Phase 4). When an LEA has no one to serve as a mentor, it may be necessary for a new headteacher to seek support from someone in another authority.

Another implication from the phases that relate to the needs of beginning headteachers is the fact that knowing about this predictable progression might help you in thinking about your life as a school leader at some point in the future. For example, it is important for you to recognize that it is understandable that the next few years on the job might find you spending a lot of time and energy thinking about personal needs. That is important. Numerous novice headteachers have expressed anxiety and almost a sense of guilt over the fact that they were not accomplishing as much as they wanted to as quickly as they had hoped. They were not becoming the effective instructional leaders suggested as goals in the research literature. Instead, they felt as if most of their time was being invested in personal concerns.

The first few years are likely to be the ones in which individuals establish their own sense of identity and comfort in their roles. As one new head once said, "I can't get too concerned about changing the world until I get my own house in order". It is perfectly understandable that you are probably not getting too involved with thoughts of torch passing (Phase 4) just yet. On the other hand, you may be tempted to feel guilty about not getting involved in more than personal interests. After all, in many cases new headteachers are alone as novices in their LEAs, and as a result it is not unusual to feel apart from colleagues and not completely committed to the goals and objectives identified by the authority. As more than one beginning head has noted over the years, "Before I become a great instructional leader, I just want to get through each day of my first year on the job."

Each new headteacher will have to establish his or her own realistic schedule that will permit movement from one phase to another. Some people will be able to move very quickly during the first few weeks of service from simply coming on board (Phase 1) to Phase 2, in which they are already looking for ways of improving the overall programmes for pupils, staff, parents and the entire community. This might be based on a variety of factors, such as the nature of their staff, what they learned as deputies and so forth. Some people may need more than a year to go beyond initial culture shock and progress beyond the coming on board phase (Phase 1).

The important thing is that any new headteacher needs to remember that time spent as a novice is valuable time in terms of a long-term career. Do not rush too quickly towards trying to learn a whole new system and changing the world in one month simply because the research on effective schools says that headteachers must make an immediate difference. It simply is not going to happen overnight for everyone. And you should not get discouraged if you do not understand everything as quickly as you had hoped you might.

The key to effectiveness is not going too fast or dragging your feet waiting for the "perfect" time to promote needed change. Perhaps a very effective strategy to follow is the development of a realistic set of annual plans to guide your work. This is an organized way to initiate change while allowing you to look at your school objectively. This type of planning might begin during your second year as a head, and it probably ought to continue throughout your career. On the following pages, I have provided an outline for this type of systematic planning.

Developing a Personal Timetable for Action

A critical part of preparing a personal professional development portfolio and action plan involves not only stating what you plan to do, but even more important, when you are going to do things. The last section of this chapter proposes that you develop a personal timetable that you will follow as you set out to meet certain professional targets during your first year on the job. Remember, you cannot accomplish everything at once, but you never accomplish anything without a serious plan to determine which things are to happen first. Another helpful tip might be to make certain that you bounce these goals off a few people you trust. Seeking this type of feedback can be very useful to you in thinking about goals and priorities.

Goal 1

The first goal I hope to accomplish in this first year as a headteacher is

....

....

I hope to achieve this goal by

....

....

The latest date I expect to achieve this goal is

....

....

Goal 2

The second goal I hope to accomplish in this first year is

....

....

I hope to achieve this goal by

....

....

The latest date I expect to achieve this goal is

....

....

Goal 3

The third goal I hope to accomplish in this first year is

....

....

I hope to achieve this goal by

....

....

The latest date I expect to achieve this goal is

....

....

This chapter concludes by providing a place for you to write three goals, but this does not mean that as a first-year headteacher you should not try more than three goals. At the same time, you should not try to do too many things at once. The ultimate answer to the question of what is the right number of things for a novice to try is something that only you can provide. How much is enough, and which things should be done first, is not something that this book can prescribe. Nor is it something that your governors or your local senior education officer can dictate. It is legitimate, of course, for governing boards to charge headteachers with goals that need to be addressed. However, if your personal objective is simply to make certain that you do not do something that is contrary to what your boss tells you, then you will do little more than follow the priorities of others as much as possible.

On the other hand, what you do, when you do it, and how you do it will always be matters that come from within you and your individual set of values and beliefs. Once again, the platform exercise described earlier is critical to your success. And sharing that platform with others will do much to increase effective communication so that you can meet the expectations of others and also focus on your personal objectives with equal commitment.

11

Building a Support System

Tony Spencer had just suffered what was undoubtedly the single worst day as the headteacher of Rylands Community School. Before he had even left his house this morning, he received a telephone call from Harriet Wilson, his secretary, who told him that she had a family emergency that would make it necessary to stay at home today. The situation might call for her attention all week, in fact. When Tony arrived at school he found Noel Watkins, his caretaker, busily working to fix the front door. It had been damaged in some heavy winds last night. Next, while Tony was working with a supply secretary to orientate her to the front office routine of the day, the phone rang almost endlessly. In less than five minutes Tony received word that two teachers were going to be late and three more were ill and would not be in at all today. Supply teachers would be needed. That was fine, except Tony knew that supply teachers would be difficult to find this week. A recent outbreak of influenza in the area was affecting all the local industries and schools which were reporting high pupil absence rates. This was going to be one of those days when "creative class coverage" would take effect. Tony knew he would be in the classroom most of the morning.

Taking over classes from time to time was something that Tony enjoyed. In fact, he missed the traditional image of the headteacher working with children in classes each day. Today was a perfect example of why the traditional image was now rare in British schools. Tony knew that, after his turn as a supply teacher, he would have to meet with a group of parents who were planning a fund raising event for the school in the spring. And he had an appointment that afternoon with Dr Edmond Carter, a testing consultant from DfES who would be in the school to talk about some new approaches to data analysis. Both of these things had to be done today. Two of the school governors had expressed a keen interest in the testing process, and Tony would be meeting with them after dinner this evening.

While Tony was thinking about things that were scheduled in his diary, he was suddenly interrupted by his secretary for today who told him that two youngsters had been brought to the front office by a teacher who had found them fighting near the school. Tony went to see what this was all about and was shocked to learn that one of the two combatants was the son of the head of his governing body! This meant that not only would he spend some time this afternoon providing some discipline to a child, but also the day had taken on a direction that might have serious political consequences.

At the end of the day Tony was driving home and began to think of this evening's activities. For one thing, he would be the chef tonight for the family. His wife had had to go to London for business early this morning, and her return train would not come back until approximately 7 pm. He also knew that he would have to have a chat with his son about some of the grades he was getting in a few of his subjects at the secondary school. And Tony kept reviewing the likely consequences of the encounter he had had this afternoon with the son of his governing board leader. Tomorrow also promised to be a challenge. He already knew that several staff members would be gone again due to illness or attendance at a conference at the LEA.

* * *

Do the things that happened to Tony sound familiar? Perhaps you have been lucky enough not to have had a single day quite as bad as his. Or maybe the day that Tony experienced was actually an easy day on your calendar. The point is that all headteachers, regardless of experience, level of school (primary or secondary), size of school, or any other variable that might be introduced, have very important, difficult and demanding jobs. And the fact is that the job will become even more demanding, critical and stressful in the future. As governmental reforms of education continue to take root, the spotlight will be directed even more on the headteacher's role in providing effective leadership. This fact must be recognized along with the other types of demands, expectations and pressures that are being placed on all educators. Who could possibly imagine that primary heads would someday be involved with crisis management plans in the wake of school shooting incidents that now seem to be a daily headline in newspapers all over the world? And what about the need to work effectively with youngsters who walk into school each day from homes where parents are child abusers, drug dealers, or other forms of felons and sociopaths?

The listing of problems faced by modern headteachers ends here. For one thing, continuing to list all the problems may cause you to begin to question your decision about becoming a headteacher in the first place. Quite simply, the benefits of being a headteacher will probably far outweigh the problems and frustrations in the long run. Nevertheless, it is critical both for immediate survival and long-term success that you find some strategies to make certain that when the alligators are nipping at your ankles, you don't get swallowed up. Even Tony was looking forward to the uncertainties and challenges of the next day.

This chapter offers a few strategies that have been identified by many very successful (and surviving) headteachers who have learned how to cope with the numerous frustrations and pressures they experience on the job. You may have already adopted some of the suggestions on your own and, in that case, you may be well beyond the advice that is offered here. Or you may be in that unfortunate state where the problems and crises have been coming along so rapidly that you have not had much time to look up from your desk and find any useful survival strategies. In that case, this chapter could be extremely important.

Strategy 1: Finding a Mentor

The single most powerful thing a new headteacher (and even experienced headteachers) can do to enhance personal survival and effectiveness is to find at least one other experienced educational leader who can be available to share expertise related to doing the job more effectively and, perhaps even more importantly, help you understand yourself and your personal transition into the headship more completely. A mentor can also help significantly with the complex task of becoming effectively socialized both into the overall profession of the headship and also into the norms, culture, practices and procedures of the school in which you now find yourself.

Do you already have at least one mentor who is helping you during this initial introduction to the headship? If so, who is it and what are some of the characteristics you have found in that person that make him or her particularly valuable to you as a mentor?

....

....

....

....

....

....

Research on mentors for headteachers has found the following characteristics of individuals frequently identified as effective mentors to aspiring and beginning headteachers. (Compare these qualities with ones you have listed above.)

- Mentors are experienced headteachers who are regarded by peers and others as effective
- Mentors demonstrate qualities of effective leaders, such as
  — good communication skills
  — intelligence
  — clear vision of what could be
  — positive interpersonal skills and sensitivity
- Mentors ask the right questions; they do not simply provide the right answers
- Mentors accept others' ways of doing things; they do not want everyone else to do it their way
- Mentors desire other people to go beyond their present levels of performance
- Mentors model principles of continuous learning and reflection
- Mentors exhibit awareness of the political and social realities of life in at least one school system

You may have noticed the absence of some other characteristics that a lot of people have often assumed to be desirable for mentors. For example, many people assume that the most effective mentors are those with many years of experience as headteachers, as if survival on the job automatically results in wisdom and insight. Clearly, such experience is not always tied to effectiveness as a mentor. Some individuals may spend 20 years as head-teachers, but unfortunately they have done the same thing for 20 years in a row! Consequently, they have not grown, and they have not learned from their own past experiences. What are you likely to gain from working with people like this?

People also assume that men must mentor men and only women can mentor women. Although people often express a desire to have same-gender mentoring relationships (and for some reason these are often easier to carry out), no research shows conclusively that men cannot be effective mentors to women (or vice versa). This is a comforting finding if one assumes that women are underrepresented in the world of secondary headships.

People also incorrectly assume that only older individuals can serve effectively as mentors to younger colleagues. Perhaps this image comes from the traditional view that the only thing a mentor does is fill up the protégé with a lot of tricks of the trade and lessons from the past. This is a very limited view of mentoring and one with the potential of being more harmful than helpful to your career. The reason is that in many cases new headteachers have been hired precisely because of the desire to get some new blood and new thinking in a school. There has been for too long a history of doing the same things in the same ways. Mentors who see themselves only as people who help you do your job in an easier way may be inadvertently limiting your future potential success by telling you "how we have always done it here".

Now that you have considered these additional issues regarding effective mentoring relationships, who are some individuals you might identify as potentially effective mentors for you as a new headteacher? (These may or may not be the same people you thought of at the beginning of this chapter.)

....

....

....

....

....

....

Strategy 2: Developing Networks

Another strategy to help you in the first years of the headship is to develop networks with other educational leaders. This can take several forms. For example, if you are one of several novice headteachers in a region, you may wish to get in contact with these other inexperienced heads to form some kind of contact for mutual support. You may wish to agree to get together once a month for a social gathering during which you can share some of your experiences about your life as a beginner. You will no doubt be surprised to learn that many of the "mistakes" that you believe that you have made are ones made by a good many of these colleagues (and more experienced colleagues as well).

Do you know of any other beginning headteachers in your area with whom you might be able to form a mutual support network?

....

....

....

....

....

....

Networks have also been formed among women headteachers. Only a few years ago this was a rarity. Now, women headteacher networks have appeared in different parts of the country, generally based on the assumption that the headship has traditionally been a man's game. As a result, it is viewed as critical to develop mutually supportive arrangements among those who want to "join the club". The same logic has been shared in the establishment of networks for representatives of ethnic and racial minority groups.

The formation of networks is an important form of potential support that may assist you in the earliest stages of your career, with an important exception. In some cases, the primary goal of a network seems to be only to maintain itself, not necessarily to provide support to individual participants. It is likely that as one matures in a professional role, it will be less important to maintain membership in a mutual support arrangement, whether the arrangement is classified as mentoring or a network. In those cases, it is important that you feel free to determine your own continuing membership. A relationship of any kind is no longer healthy when participants feel as if they are forced to continue to stay involved.

Strategy 3: Staying in Touch with National Developments

The UK has seen many developments in the area of school management in recent years. As a new headteacher, you may wish to keep informed of many different activities which are likely to provide some considerable support to you during your career. Among the most notable actions have been the creation of the National College for School Leadership, Annual Performance Reviews, National Professional Qualifications for Headteachers (NPQH), and Headteachers in Post (HIP).

National College for School Leadership

Since 1998, the National College for School Leadership in Nottingham has worked toward the creation of a unified set of programmes available to serve the needs of current and future school leaders across the nation. NCSL has been responsible for creating numerous programmes designed to assist headteachers in developing their skills needed to ensure effective school improvement efforts. These have included a large number of conferences, instructional materials, and technology that has been made available to school leaders.

Annual Performance Reviews

One of the things that Tony Spencer in our opening scenario was facing on his very busy day was preparing for his Annual Performance Review that day. Like many heads, he was not looking forward to the next day's appointment with his review governors and the external advisor assigned to him. Although he had prepared the required papers for his Annual Performance Review, and he had already sent them to the governors and consultant over a month ago, he had avoided confronting the concerns about the process which had caused him real distress last year.

Tony knew from the DfEEs guidance that his achievements should be acknowledged in addition to new targets being "agreed". But it had not turned out that way. He left his three-hour meeting feeling quite undervalued and inadequate, despite knowing that according to informal comments from his LEA link inspector and some governors that he had made a good start as the new head at Rylands School. A year later, he was wondering how he could avoid a re-run of last year's unbalanced review meeting.

The headteacher's Annual Performance Review is a requirement of governors and the headteacher, and it informs a separate process, namely the governors' review of the head's salary. It is therefore a most significant formal assessment process each year for all heads. The purpose of the review process is to give governors an opportunity to formally prioritise and review the work of he head. The targets that are set, ideally through conversations with the head, are to be a sub-set of the work that the head will undertake during the year. Normally the review meeting consists of a review of progress made toward last year's targets and an assessment of the head's effectiveness. This is followed by a discussion of five or six new targets and also monitoring arrangements for the year.

It is understandable that heads often feel anxious about these annual meetings which normally place the headteacher alone in a room with three governors and the external advisor. But these sessions can also be useful ways in which the headteacher can begin to craft a personal vision of what he or she wishes to see in the school. And in this way, those who are the reviewers can begin to serve as valuable resources to both experienced and new headteachers.

First, it is important to recall that you are the lead professional in the school. Your governors, although technically your "board of directors", are unlikely to be education experts. As a result, you may wish to begin your Annual Performance Review by meeting first with your external advisor. In this way, the annual meeting is likely to proceed more smoothly and enable some tentative decisions to be made in advance of the formal meeting with governors.

During the formal review meeting, do not hesitate to make use of the session to garner needed support for your plans and vision of where to take the school in the future. You need to be explicit regarding your new targets. This can be an important learning opportunity for your governors who can be enlisted to provide support without necessarily beginning to micro-manage the daily operation of your school.

You may wish to think through your "script" for use with those involved with your Annual Review. For example, what is the key evidence of your achievements in the past that you will share with your review governors at your Annual Review meetings?

Evidence for Target 1

....

....

....

....

....

....

Evidence for Target 2

....

....

....

....

....

....

Evidence for Target 3

....

....

....

....

....

....

Evidence for Target 4

....

....

....

....

....

....

Evidence for Target 5

....

....

....

....

....

....

Outline your suggestions for aspects for your work that can become legitimate targets for the coming year:

Leadership and management

....

....

....

....

....

....

Pupil progress

....

....

....

....

....

....

....

....

Other issues, including your personal professional development

....

....

....

....

....

....

As a way to realize the full potential of the Annual Performance Review, make sure to stay in touch with the review governors during the year by agreeing progress-monitoring arrangements. This is an opportunity to share your achievements on an ongoing basis, and also a way to explain any changes which might impede progress. When the time for your next Annual Review arrives, there should be no surprises for you or for your governors.

Outline how you will keep your review governors in touch with your progress over the next 12 months.

....

....

....

....

....

....

National Professional Qualifications for Headteachers (NPQH) and HIP

There are three main stages to NPQH: access, development and final stages. The route candidates take through these stages will be determined by assessment, on the basis of prior experience and training needs. The programme will receive further revisions with effect from September 2003; NPQH is mandatory for newly appointed heads from April 2003.

There are three routes through the programme which allow staff at differing stages of experience and development to enter the scheme.

Route 1

Candidates with limited senior management experience will begin at the access stage and, depending on their needs, they will study one or more of the four access modules before proceeding to the development stage. The access stage will be mainly undertaken by self-study, but also includes two days of face-to-face training and on-line learning activities.

Route 2

Candidates with broad senior management experience but who wish to confirm their knowledge and skills in some areas and extend them in others, will begin at the development stage. They attend an induction day and arrange for a tutor to visit them in school to agree their personal training and development plan and the focus of their work on school improvement. They will then undertake training on the four modules of the development stage, a tutor will visit the candidate in school for a day to assess whether they are ready to proceed to the final stage.

Route 3

The fast pathway to the final stage is intended for candidates who have substantial experience of a range of aspects of school leadership and who are able to assemble evidence of this. Candidates will attend an induction day and arrange for a tutor to visit them in school to discuss and confirm whether this is the most appropriate route for them. If Route 3 is confirmed, candidates will then prepare for a tutor to visit them in school.

HIP will replace the former Headlamp from September 2003. The idea is that heads will carry with them a Leadership Development Profile from their NPQH experience and extend this through involvement with the HIP programme.

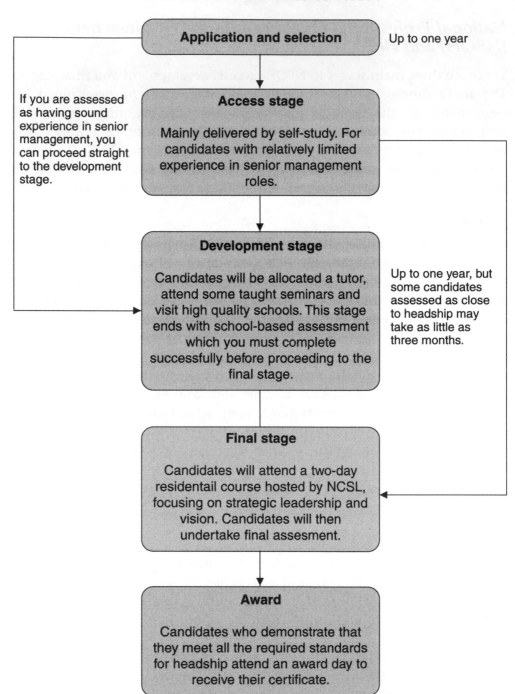

Figure 11.1 The stages to NPQH

HIP will include an initial needs assessment and a further assessment during the three years of the programme. Modules will be selected in relation to need and will cover such areas as raising achievement, transformational leadership, coaching and mentoring. Training will be provided by a number of approved providers and funding is likely to be made available to schools.

Strategy 4: Maintaining Personal and Family Support

A fourth form of support may be the most obvious one, but it is often overlooked as people embark upon new careers. Often the best way to find your feet in a new situation is by drawing on your natural, immediate environment. As you begin your career as a headteacher, it is likely that your world will be filled with so many new responsibilities, people, and activities that you will become overwhelmed with many competing demands and interests. Suddenly, things and events that were important to you only a few months ago seem distant and less important as you work hard to develop a new professional identity and self-image. Although that is understandable, it is critical to keep a personal focus on what is truly important in your life. Demands of a professional nature are important; the roots and foundation in your personal and family life are even more important and will be with you well beyond your career as a headteacher.

The first recommendation, then, is to make certain that, whenever possible, you do whatever is needed and reasonable to retain some sense of normality in your personal life. Do not ignore family and friends. Do not forget your son's piano recital or your daughter's swimming meeting. Remember that the annual family trip to the Lake District or France was a big part of your life when you were a classroom teacher; it is still a part of your life now that you are a primary headteacher. Return phone calls to personal friends who knew you "in olden times", before you were such an important person. In short, keep your compass and your perspective; do not forget what is really important to you. And remember that you can be a very effective headteacher even if you take a night off to watch a very bad film or read a novel just for entertainment.

The second recommendation is related to your need to maintain your health. Critically ill headteachers are not terribly effective. Do not neglect matters of health, personal fitness and well-being. This is important with respect to matters of physical well-being and also emotional, intellectual and even spiritual health. Go to the doctor when you are sick and for regular examinations, exercise, eat right (and do not fall into the "headteacher-as-martyr" syndrome that seemingly rewards people for never having lunch, skipping breakfast, and living on coffee all day) and take care of your body. Get out of your office, forget about your work once in a while, read a book for pleasure, attend a concert, or do any of a thousand things that will remind you of your need to get out of your role as an educational leader on occasion.

With regard to intellectual well-being, do something that challenges your mental capacity. Some headteachers make it a practice to attend lectures at local universities, or they participate in study groups that have nothing to do with the field of education as a way to keep their minds sharp; they enrol in language courses or other programmes that seemingly have nothing to do with schools as a way to keep contact with their spiritual core. And with regard to spiritual well-being, if you have always been involved with church-related activities, is there any reason to stop this involvement simply because you have the title "headteacher" on your door?

It is not possible to prescribe all the things that you might do to ensure that you maintain a balance in your priorities as a new headteacher. I am not suggesting that the only route to happiness and success will be to maintain a perfect family life. After all, headteachers have situations in their personal lives during which traditional patterns of home and happiness might be changed or interrupted. And those situations might have nothing to do with their effectiveness as a headteacher or their personal well-being. At times it will be impossible to get to the gym, play a round of golf, or attend the opera. The critical message here is that it is not only a good idea but in some ways a critical responsibility for headteachers to think of their own personal needs above other issues.

Developing a Plan of Action

This chapter and this book conclude by asking you to plan a systematic way of putting into effect many of the support mechanisms identified here. It is extremely important to select some clear ways in which you might reasonably expect to enjoy greater success in your job. By taking time to write out some of the sources of support you may find for yourself, you will become committed to these various approaches and activities.

Strategy 1: Find a Mentor

Who are some individuals who could serve in a mentoring capacity to you as you move into the headship?

....

....

....

....

....

....

What are some of the specific concerns associated with your work as a headteacher that you believe might be addressed by a mentoring relationship?

....

....

....

....

....

....

Strategy 2: Develop Networks

Do you currently have any networks developed with other headteachers?

....

....

....

....

....

....

In what specific ways might your network assist you in dealing with concerns and issues you face as a beginning headteacher?

....

....

....

....

....

....

Strategy 3: Staying in Touch with National Developments

Indicate how you believe that the annual mandatory process can assist you in achieving personal and professional goals each year:

....

....

....

....

....

....

Strategy 4: Maintain Personal and Family Support

List some of the ways you intend to spend more time with your family, engage in leisure activities, or simply take care of yourself during the next several months.

....

....

....

....

....

....

What are some of the personal and professional benefits you hope to achieve?

....

....

....

....

....

....

Index